Wacky Wordbook of

VOCABULARY BOOSTERS

PENGUIN BOOKS

PENGUIN BOOKS

Penguin Books is part of the Penguin Random House group of companies
whose addresses can be found at global.penguinrandomhouse.com

Published by Penguin Random House SEA Pte Ltd
40 Penjuru Lane, #03-12, Block 2
Singapore 609216

First published in Penguin Books by Penguin Random House SEA 2025

Designer credit: Neha Singh
Content contributor : Tanushree Banerjee

10 9 8 7 6 5 4 3 2 1

ISBN: 9789815323344

Printed at Replika Press Pvt. Ltd, India

www.penguin.sg

Contents

WHIMSICAL WORDS

1. Bumfuzzle

buhm-fuhz-uh-l

Meaning: to confuse, perplex or bewilder someone

Sentence: The tricky question bumfuzzled me.

2. Fiddle-dee-dee

fidel-dee-dee

Meaning: an expression of mock or disapproval

Sentence: The weather girl warned us about the storm. My brother just said, 'Fiddle-dee-dee,' and dragged us outside on the porch.

3. Codswallop

kawdz-vaw-luhp

Meaning: nonsense talk or something utterly ridiculous and untrue

Sentence: Martin said that the rumor was just codswallop, and no one should believe it.

4. Raconteur

ra-kawn-tuh

Meaning: a person who is skilled in telling stories in an amusing or entertaining way

Sentence: Cameron is the life of the party, for he is such a raconteur.

5. Gobsmacked

gob-smakt

Meaning: utterly astonished or amazed

Sentence: I was gobsmacked finding out about the medal that Roy got for just participating in the Comic Con.

6. Brouhaha

bru-ha-ha

Meaning: a noisy and overexcited reaction

Sentence: The argument over the design of the cake caused quite a brouhaha at the bakery.

7. Doozy

du-zi

Meaning: something outstanding or remarkable

Sentence: The thunderstorm last night was a real doozy.

8. Gadzooks

gaed-zuks

Meaning: an exclamation of surprise or annoyance

Sentence: Gadzooks! That poor fella slipped on the icy lake.

9. Skullduggery

skuhl-duh-guh-ree

Meaning: underhanded or deceitful behavior

Sentence: The Sheriff uncovered Paul's skullduggery during the theft investigation.

10. Baloney

buh-loh-nee

Meaning: nonsense or foolishness

Sentence: Susan is just making up silly stories; it is pure baloney.

11. Dillydally

dil-i dal-i

Meaning: to waste time by being indecisive or hesitant

Sentence: Miss Perkins is a straight-talking teacher with little patience for dilly-dallying.

12. Goober

gu-ber

Meaning: a foolish or clumsy person

Sentence: Helen is such a goober for spilling coffee all over the kitchen counter.

13. Higgledy-piggledy

hig-el-di pig-el-di

Meaning: in a disorganized or chaotic manner

Sentence: Mariam's art project is a work of her higgledy-piggledy attitude.

14. Ballyhoo

bael-i-hu

Meaning: extravagant promotion or publicity

Sentence: The ballyhoo over Macy's parade amuses me.

15. Piffle

pif-uhl

Meaning: nonsense or trivial talk

Sentence: Jessica is known for her piffle.

16. Whippersnapper

vip-uh-snap-uh

Meaning: a young and inexperienced person who is arrogant or cheeky

Sentence: My teacher scolded the whippersnapper for disrespecting his classmates.

17. Lickety-split

lik-e-ti-split

Meaning: at great speed or quickly

Sentence: Sally and Paul run lickety-split to get their favorite snacks from the kitchen.

18. Hoopla

hu-p-la

Meaning: exaggerated or excessive excitement

Sentence: The magician brought so much hoopla to Ryan's birthday party, with colorful ribbons, pigeons, and abracadabra everywhere.

19. Noodle

nu-del

Meaning: a slang used for a simpleton or silly person

Sentence: Janice is such a noodle trying to drink milk with a spoon.

20. Snickerpuff

sni-kur-puf

Meaning: a playful way of describing a silly laugh or giggle

Sentence: When Uncle John tripped over the toy, James let out a little snickerpuff.

21. Whatchamacallit

wat-cha-me-ka-lit

Meaning: a term used when one cannot remember or does not know the name of something

Sentence: Please pass the… whatchamacallit kept on the table.

22. Bazinga

bae-zihn-gae

Meaning: a term used to indicate that someone has been tricked or pranked

Sentence: Bazinga! Sheldon has been tricked by Leonard.

23. Nudiustertian

nu-di-us-ter-tian

Meaning: the day before yesterday

Sentence: I went to Herman Park nudiustertian and saw children playing on the swings and taking train rides.

24. Cattywampus

kaet-i-wum-pus

Meaning: crooked, askew, or disorganized

Sentence:
After the hurricane, the entire village was cattywampus.

25. Absquatulate

ab-skwoch-uh-leyt

Meaning: to leave abruptly, in a sneaky way

Sentence: When my bunny heard the oven ding, it quickly absquatulated from the room, seeking refuge under the couch.

26. Taradiddle

tar-ra-did-dle

Meaning: a trivial or insignificant lie

Sentence: Don't believe Maurice's taradiddle about seeing a ghost in the woods. She likes to make up silly stories.

27. Razzle-dazzle

raez-el daez-el

Meaning: exciting or showy activity

Sentence: The magician's act was full of razzle-dazzle, but no real magic.

28. Widdershins

wid-uhr-shinz

Meaning: moving in a counterclockwise direction

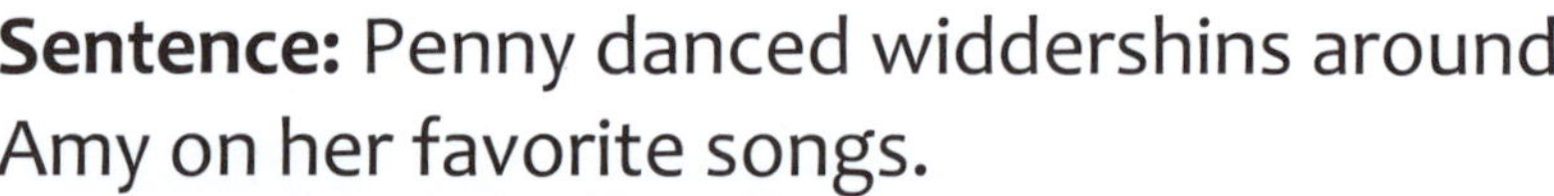

Sentence: Penny danced widdershins around Amy on her favorite songs.

29. Skiddly-boop

skid-li-bup

Meaning: a phrase used to describe something fun or exciting

Sentence: Tintin had a skiddly-boop day at the granny's house, full of board games and delicious chocolate pudding.

30. Yerk

yurk

Meaning: to move or pull with a sudden sharp motion

Sentence: Timmy yerked at Harry's arm so hard that it started to pain.

31. Flibbertigibbet

fli-buh-tee-ji-buht

Meaning: a foolish and overly talkative person

Sentence: Terry is charming but she is a bit of a flibbertigibbet as well.

32. Bricolage

bree-koh-lahj

Meaning: creation from a diverse range of available things; a work of art made from mixed materials

Sentence: Her college dorm was a bricolage of memories, with photos, cut-outs and magazine covers from the four years of college.

33. Yex

yeks

Meaning: an old word for hiccuping or sobbing with gasps

Sentence: Sharon gave out a loud yex during the seminar.

34. Bumbershoot

buhm-ber-shoot

Meaning: an old-fashioned word for an umbrella

Sentence: Holland borrowed Janine's bumbershoot before heading out into the rainforest.

35. Scurryfunge

skuhr-ee-fuhnj

Meaning: a hasty tidying of a house when a visitor is expected

Sentence: She scurryfunged the living room when she got a text saying her friend would come over in five minutes.

36. Skedaddle

skuh-da-dl

Meaning: to leave hurriedly or quickly

Sentence: Upon hearing the tornado alert, we skedaddled back to the house.

37. Blubber

bla-b-er

Meaning: to cry noisily and uncontrollably

Sentence: Susan started to blubber on the refusal of the last piece of cake.

FANTASTICAL & PLAYFUL WORDS

38. Bombastic

bam-bes-tik

Meaning: overly pretentious language meant to sound important but lacking real substance

Sentence: The minister's bombastic speech held no truth.

39. Befuddled

bi-fad-eld

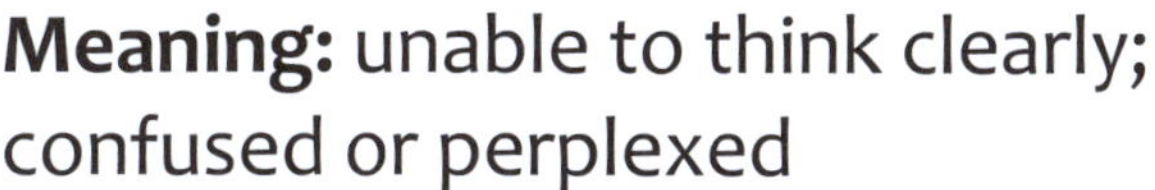

Meaning: unable to think clearly; confused or perplexed

Sentence: Jenna was exhausted after the meeting; she was befuddled with tons of information.

40. Fantasia

fan-tay-zhuh

Meaning: a magical, imaginative world; a composition or work of art that is free-flowing

Sentence: Disney World is a fantasia of wonder and magic where Ron can live his dream of becoming a prince.

41. Groak

gro-hk

Meaning: to silently watch someone while they eat, hoping they will share

Sentence: My dog would groak every time I have steak for dinner.

42. Blatteroon

bla-tuh-roon

Meaning: an obsolete term for a person who talks too much

Sentence: Mario is such a blatteroon; he just doesn't stop talking about his new car.

43. Jester

jes-tur

Meaning: a funny person who entertains often with a joke in a king's court

Sentence: The jester made everyone in the royal court laugh with his silly jokes and tricks.

44. Wobblegobble

wob-ble-gob-ble

Meaning: a humorous term for eating in a shaky or clumsy manner

Sentence: Jake sat by the campfire and began to wobblegobble his soup, spilling half of it on his shirt.

45. Zimbi

zimbi

Meaning: a cowrie shell historically used as currency in parts of Africa

Sentence: Paul used zimbi to buy chocolate at the mall.

46. Snickerfritz

snik-er-fritz

Meaning: a silly or mischievous person

Sentence: Penny is such a snickerfritz always making funny faces at the elders.

47. Umpty

uhmp-tee

Meaning: signifies a large, indefinite number

Sentence: Mother asked Bonny umpty times to shut the windows at night.

48. Mimblewimble

Mim-bul-Wim-bul

Meaning: a magical spell or trick

Sentence: The scary witch said a mimblewimble to fire up the pot of potions.

49. Quibblequack

kwib-ble-kwack

Meaning: a playful argument or squabble

Sentence: The penguins had a quibblequack about who would jump off the cliff into the ocean.

50. Wamblecropt

wam-buhl-kropt

Meaning: rumbling stomach

Sentence: Jenna will be wamblecropt if she doesn't stop eating the fiery snacks.

51. Fizzlebop

fiz-uhl-bop

Meaning: a fun word to describe a lively activity

Sentence: Playing fetch with my dog Simba is a fizzlebop of running and laughing.

52. Ditty

di-ti

Meaning: a light-hearted, short, and simple song

Sentence: I enjoyed the ditty under the moonlight.

53. Fuddy-duddy

fuh-dee-duh-dee

Meaning: an old-fashioned, overly conservative, or unimaginative person, often resistant to change

Sentence: Grandpa is a bit of a fuddy-duddy when it comes to technology.

54. Cockalorum

kah-kuh-lor-um

Meaning: a boastful and self-important person

Sentence: Deedee is such a cockalorum trying to find faults with everything.

55. Snugglepuff

snug-uhl-puff

Meaning: something cozy and a soft hug

Sentence: My granny's warm lap is a snugglepuff on a chilly night.

56. Gigglegroan

gig-ul-grohn

Meaning: a fun word describing a mix of giggling and groaning

Sentence: The pillow fight made Henry and Sammy gigglegroan in the end.

57. Revelry

rev-uhl-ree

Meaning: lively and noisy festivities

Sentence: The revelry continued late until midnight after the big win.

MYSTICAL & OBSCURE WORDS

58. Arcane

a-kein

Meaning: understood by few; mysterious or secret

Sentence: The lyrics of the song are arcane and difficult to understand.

---

59. Numinous

noo-muh-nus

Meaning: mysterious, spiritual, and filled with divine presence

Sentence: The old cathedral had a numinous glow, as if it held secrets of another world.

---

60. Hierophany

hy-ruh-fan-ee

Meaning: a manifestation of the sacred or divine

Sentence: The glowing figure in the sky was seen as a hierophany, a sign from the gods.

61. Jargogle

jar-gog-uhl

Meaning: to confuse or jumble things

Sentence: Sam is known for his jargogle at school.

---

62. Fey

fay

Meaning: giving an impression of vague unworldliness or mystery

Sentence: Shiloh's fey charm and eccentric ways gave her the top spot in the play.

---

63. Obsidian

uhb-sid-ee-uhn

Meaning: a volcanic glass, often black, used in tools, jewelry, and sometimes associated with mystical properties

Sentence: The wizard used his obsidian dagger to perform rituals.

64. Tenebrous

ten-uh-brus

Meaning: dark, shadowy, and mysterious

Sentence: The tenebrous forest seemed alive, whispering secrets in the wind.

65. Cryptonym

krip-toh-nim

Meaning: a secret or disguised name

Sentence: My neighbor lives with a cryptonym to protect his identity; I think he works for the Intelligence agency.

66. Sphinxlike

sfinks-laik

Meaning: mysterious and difficult to interpret or understand

Sentence: Monalisa's sphinxlike smile made it difficult for Ryan to understand what she was thinking.

67. Esoterica

es-uh-ter-i-kuh

Meaning: things understood by or meant for a small group of people

Sentence: The library had a section filled with esoterica about ancient rituals.

---

68. Obfuscate

ob-fuh-skayt

Meaning: to deliberately make something obscure or confusing

Sentence: The witch obfuscated her intentions with vague and gibberish language.

---

69. Enigma

uh-nig-muh

Meaning: a person, thing, or situation that is mysterious, puzzling, or difficult to understand

Sentence: She was an enigma to her coworkers, always quiet yet full of unexpected ideas.

70. Eldritch

el-dritch

Meaning: weird, sinister, or ghostly

Sentence: The eldritch sounds of the movie send shivers down the spine.

71. Stygian

stij-ee-uhn

Meaning: extremely dark, gloomy, or forbidding

Sentence: The cave's stygian surroundings were home to thousands of bats.

72. Tergiversate

ter-jiv-er-sayt

Meaning: to avoid making a clear statement

Sentence: My friend continued to tergiversate when asked about his grades in the class test.

---

73. Augury

aw-guh-ree

Meaning: a sign of what will happen in the future; an omen

Sentence: Ana's positivity amidst the hurricane was an augury of hope.

---

74. Nictitate

nikti-tayt

Meaning: to wink or blink, often in a secretive manner

Sentence: I nictitated at Weasley, but he could not understand my gestures. Alas! He blabbed our secrets to my mommy.

75. Alchemical

al-keh-muh-kl

Meaning: involving a seemingly magical process of transformation, creation, or combination

Sentence: Writing poetry is an alchemical task.

---

76. Threnody

thren-uh-dee

Meaning: a song or a poem that expresses grief or mourning

Sentence: Alex sang a threnody at the loss of his lost pet.

---

77. Kenopsia

ken-op-see-uh

Meaning: the eerie atmosphere of a place that is usually full of people but is now abandoned

Sentence: The abandoned castle's kenopsia at midnight is eerie and unsettling.

78. Esbat

ez-bat

Meaning: a meeting or gathering of witches

Sentence: Sabrina and the other witches fixed Saturday night for their weekly esbat.

79. Miasma

mai-aezme

Meaning: a highly unpleasant or unhealthy atmosphere

Sentence: I do not like the miasma of Tully's house.

80. Sibilant

sibi-lent

Meaning: hissing sound

Sentence: The movie has sibilant noises in every other scene making my heart skip a beat.

81. Phantasm

fan-taz-uhm

Meaning: a ghost or illusion, especially one created by the mind

Sentence: The carriage seemed to glide like a phantasm at midnight scaring everyone in sight.

82. Chimera

ki-mie-ra

Meaning: a thing that is wished for but is illusory or impossible to achieve

Sentence: Living on the planet Mars is no less than a chimera.

83. Quagmire

kvag-mai-uh

Meaning: a complex or hazardous situation

Sentence: The country became a quagmire after the war.

84. Cloistered

kloy-stuhd

Meaning: kept away from the outside world; sheltered

Sentence: Annabelle lived a cloistered life in mystery and silence.

---

85. Inchoate

in-koh-it

Meaning: just begun and not fully formed or developed; vague

Sentence: Lily's ideas about the school project remained inchoate until she started working on the details.

WORDS OF MAGIC

86. Rune

roon

Meaning: a letter or symbol from an ancient alphabet used in magic

Sentence: Sabrina and Raven have magical abilities to decipher the rune stones, revealing the secrets of the past.

87. Grimoire

grim-wahr

Meaning: a book of magical spells and instructions for casting them

Sentence: The wizard carefully studied the ancient grimoire to cast a spell.

88. Talisman

tal-iz-muhn

Meaning: an object thought to have magical powers to bring good luck

Sentence: Ali carried a talisman for good luck.

89. Alakazam

a-luh-kuh-zam

Meaning: a magical word often used to signify the beginning of a magical action or to prompt an instantaneous transformation

Sentence: "Alakazam! Your wish is my command," said the magician to Jason.

90. Oracle

or-uh-kuhl

Meaning: a person through whom a deity is believed to speak, giving wise or prophetic advice

Sentence: The oracle foretold Prince Julian's journey to save the kingdom.

91. Thaumaturgy

thaw-muh-tur-jee

Meaning: the capability of a magician to perform miracles or magic

Sentence: The sorcerer's thaumaturgy healed the sick with a mere touch.

92. Alacrity

uh-lak-ri-tee

Meaning: a magical quickness or eagerness to act

Sentence: With alacrity, the witch chanted the spell before the enemy could attack.

93. Voodoo

voo-doo

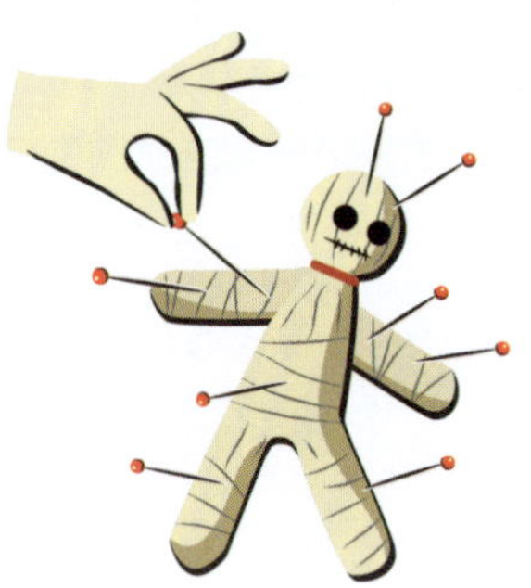

Meaning: a form of magic often associated with rituals and spiritual practices

Sentence: The villagers believed in the power of voodoo to ask the Rain God for a heavy downpour.

94. Mana

mah-nuh

Meaning: a supernatural force or energy believed to exist in certain objects or people

Sentence: The nun from our church is said to have a powerful mana.

95. Sortilege

sor-ti-lej

Meaning: the practice of foretelling the future from a card or other item drawn at random from a collection

Sentence: Since retiring, Jessica has dedicated herself to the art of sortilege, drawing cards to foresee life's events.

96. Chthonic

thon-ik

Meaning: related to the underworld or deep, hidden magical forces

Sentence: The wizard drew power from chthonic spirits that lived beneath the Earth.

97. Oneiromancy

oh-nye-roh-man-see

Meaning: the magical practice of predicting the future through dreams

Sentence: The old woman practiced oneiromancy, interpreting dreams as messages from the gods.

98. Necromancy

nek-roh-man-see

Meaning: the practice of attempting to communicate with the dead, often for divination or magical purposes

Sentence: My family does not believe in necromancy or fairy tales.

99. Leprechaun

lep-ruh-kawn

Meaning: a small, mischievous, mythical creature from Irish folklore

Sentence: The leprechaun had a pot of gold behind the iron gates of the palace.

100. Apotropaic

ap-uh-troh-pay-ik

Meaning: magic or charms used to ward off evil or bad luck

Sentence: The villagers hung apotropaic symbols on their doors to protect against curses.

---

101. Gnome

no-hm

Meaning: a small, magical creature that guards treasures underground

Sentence: The garden gnome had a purple-colored beard and a red hat.

LONG & TONGUE-TWISTING WORDS

102. Methionylthreonylthreonylglutaminylarginylisoleucine

meth-eye-oh-nil-three-oh-nil-three-oh-nil-gloo-tam-in-il-ar-jin-il...eye-so-loo-seen

Meaning: a chemical name for a type of protein

Sentence: Scientists use shorter names because methionylthreonylthreonylglutaminylarginylisoleucine is impossible to say in one breath.

103. Pneumonoultramicroscopicsilicovolcanoconiosis

nuː,mon-oul-tre,mai-kro,skop-ik,sil-i-kau,vol,kei-nou,keun-i'ou-sis

Meaning: a lung disease caused by inhaling very fine silicate or quartz dust

Sentence: Workers exposed to fine dust particles are at risk of developing pneumonoultramicroscopicsilicovolcanoconiosis.

104. Hippopotomonstrosesquipedaliophobia

hip-po-po-to-mon-stro-ses-quipped-alio-phobia

Meaning: the fear of long words

Sentence: Justin suffers from hippopotomonstrosesquipedaliophobia.

105. Hyperpolysyllabicsesquipedalianism

haiper,palisi'laek,seskwipi'deilianizem

Meaning: the tendency to use very long, multi-syllabic words

Sentence: His hyperpolysyllabicsesquipedalianism was both impressive and exhausting to listen to.

106. Supercalifragilisticexpialidocious

su:-pe-kael-i,fraedg-i,lis-tik,ek-spi,el-i'dou-es

Meaning: something fantastic or extraordinary

Sentence: When Jasmine saw the magic castle, she exclaimed, “This is absolutely supercalifragilisticexpialidocious!”

107. Pseudopseudohypoparathyroidism

soo-doh-soo-doh-hahy-poh-par-uh-thahy-royd-iz-uhm

Meaning: a genetic disorder

Sentence: Loretta’s pseudopseudohypoparathyroidism was diagnosed by a specialist.

108. Floccinaucinihilipilification

flok-si-naw-si-nahy-hi-li-pil-i-fi-kay-shuhn

Meaning: the act of estimating something as worthless

Sentence: Ron's floccinaucinihilipilification of granny's paintings offended everyone in the family.

---

109. Antidisestablishmentarianism

aen-tiˌdis-iˌstaeb-lee-sh-men-tae-ri-aˌni-zem

Meaning: opposition to the disestablishment of the Church of England

Sentence: The debate on church reignited memories of antidisestablishmentarianism in England.

---

110. Spectrophotofluorometrically

pek-troh-pho-to-fluor-oh-met-rik-lee

Meaning: related to measuring light emitted by substances

Sentence: The lab analyzed the sample spectrophotofluorometrically to check its properties.

111. Honorificabilitudinitatibus

hon-oh-rif-ih-kab-il-it-yoo-din-it-at-ih-bus

Meaning: the state of being able to receive honors

Sentence: The teacher boasted about his honorificabilitudinitatibus after receiving the 'Best Teacher' award.

112. Psychoneuroendocrinological

sy-koh-nu-ro-en-do-kri-no-loj-i-kul

Meaning: related to the connection between the brain, nervous system, and hormone

Sentence: The study of stress involves psychoneuroendocrinological research.

113. Electroencephalographically

ee-lek-tro-en-sef-uh-low-graf-ik-lee

Meaning: related to recording brain's electrical activity

Sentence: The doctors monitored the patient electroencephalographically to check for seizures.

114. Transcendentalistically

tran-sen-den-tal-is-ti-klee

Meaning: deep philosophical or spiritual thought

Sentence: He spoke transcendentalistically about the meaning of life and the universe.

---

115. Otorhinolaryngologist

oh-toh-rye-noh-lar-in-gol-uh-jist

Meaning: a doctor specializing in the ear, nose, and throat

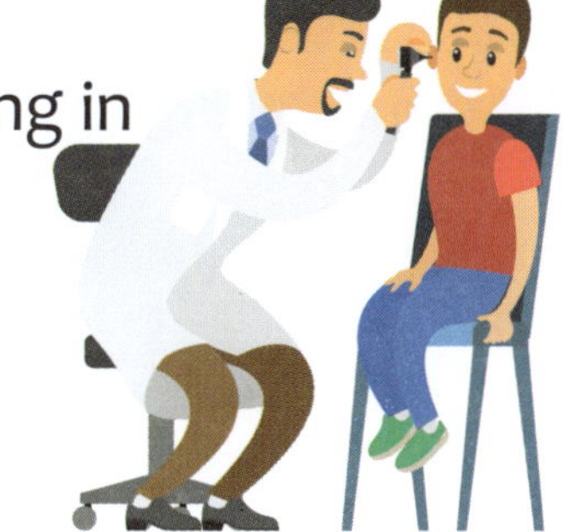

Sentence: Mommy took me to an otorhinolaryngologist to treat my throat infection.

---

116. Dodecahedronalization

doh-dek-uh-hee-droh-nal-iz-ay-shun

Meaning: the process of turning something into a twelve-sided shape

Sentence: The 3D artist performed dodecahedronalization on the cube to make it more complex.

117. Polyphiloprogenitive

pol-ee-fil-oh-proh-jen-uh-tiv

Meaning: extremely prolific in producing ideas

Sentence: The polyphiloprogenitive director staged four new plays in one year.

---

118. Transmogrification

trans-mog-rih-fi-kay-shuhn

Meaning: the act of changing into a different form

Sentence: The story ended with transmogrification of the frog to a handsome prince.

---

119. Sesquipedalianism

ses-kwi-pi-day-lee-uh-niz-uhm

Meaning: the tendency to use long words

Sentence: His habit of sesquipedalianism made his speeches hard to understand.

120. Phantasmagorical

fan-taz-muh-gor-i-kul

Meaning: having a fantastic appearance, like a dream

Sentence: We reached the phantasmagorical landscape after two hours of uphill trekking.

---

121. Anthropomorphism

an-thruh-puh-mawr-fiz-uhm

Meaning: giving human traits to animals or objects

Sentence: Shaun exhibits anthropomorphism with his action figures.

---

122. Quinquagenarian

kwin-kwuh-juh-nair-ee-uhn

Meaning: a person in their fifties

Sentence: Aunt Lydia is a quinquagenarian celebrating her 54th birthday.

123. Hapax legomenon

hay-paks luh-gom-uh-non

Meaning: a word or expression that occurs only once in a text or book

Sentence: The ancient manuscript contained a hapax legomenon that puzzled the historians.

---

124. Prognostication

prog-nos-ti-kay-shuhn

Meaning: predicting future events

Sentence: Joe's prognostication of an earthquake caused panic in the family.

---

125. Tergiversation

tur-jiv-er-say-shuhn

Meaning: the act of changing loyalties or abandoning a cause

Sentence: Fiona's tergiversation shocked her team as she played for the opposing team.

126. Consanguineous

kawn-sang-gwin-ee-uhs

Meaning: of the same blood or origin; specifically descended from the same ancestor

Sentence: Ron felt just as close to his adopted brother as he did to his two consanguineous siblings.

---

127. Surreptitious

sur-up-tish-us

Meaning: kept secret, especially because it would not be approved of

Sentence: Uncle Joe and daddy had a surreptitious meeting in the garage.

HISTORICAL WORDS

128. Absolution

ab-suh-loo-shun

Meaning: a historical term in Christianity referring to the forgiveness of sins

Sentence: The priest gave absolution to those who confessed to their sins.

---

129. Quisling

kwiz-ling

Meaning: derived from Vidkun Quisling, a historical figure in World War II Norway; traitor who collaborates with an enemy force

Sentence: Tom was labeled a quisling for betraying his team during the game at the arcade.

---

130. Antebellum

an-ti-'bel-uhm

Meaning: existing before a war, especially the American Civil War

Sentence: South Carolina is a state of charming antebellum houses.

131. Wyrd

wee-rd

Meaning: an old concept of fate or destiny, particularly in Anglo-Saxon belief

Sentence: Shaun changed his wyrd through acts of courage.

---

132. Pannychis

pa-nik-is

Meaning: an ancient term referring to an all-night feast or ceremony

Sentence: The villagers held a pannychis to celebrate the end of the harvest.

133. Epoch

ee-pok

Meaning: a period marked by a significant event

Sentence: The invention of the Internet marked a new epoch in communication.

134. Nativism

ney-tiv-iz-uhm

Meaning: a belief of favoring native inhabitants over immigrants

Sentence: A few leaders have opposed the rise of nativism in their countries.

135. Schism

skiz-uhm

Meaning: a split or division of a group into opposing factions, such as the Great Schism of Christianity

Sentence: The schism in the team put me in the awkward position of having to choose one over the other.

136. Bourgeoisie

boo-uhzh-vaa-zee

Meaning: people who own capital, such as land, factories and raw materials; historically, this term refers to the middle or capitalist class

Sentence: The rise of the bourgeoisie was seen at the end of the eighteenth century.

137. Mendicant

men-di-kant

Meaning: refers to a beggar, often in historical contexts, denoting a specific social role

Sentence: Despite his wealthy upbringing, his mendicant lifestyle puzzled his friends.

138. Geste

jest

Meaning: refers to a notable deed or gesture, often used in historical or chivalric contexts

Sentence: The dresser acclaimed Mary's action as a kindly geste.

139. City-State

sit-ee-steit

Meaning: a term used in ancient history for a city that governs itself and the surrounding area independently

Sentence: There are free showers for the homeless in public bathrooms in the city-state.

140. Zax

zaks

Meaning: an old, specialized tool used by roofers for cutting and shaping roof slates

Sentence: My dad is an expert in using the zax, and dressing the roof perfectly.

141. Schmaltz

shmahlts

Meaning: an ancient term for excessive sentimentality

Sentence: Jennifer is full of schmaltz, crying over every lost mark in her test.

142. Besom

bee-zuhm

Meaning: a stiff broom made out of sticks and twigs tied together

Sentence: I saw a picture of my great-great grandmother sweeping withered leaves with a besom.

143. Vomitorium

vah-muh-tawr-ee-uhm

Meaning: entrance or exit passages in an ancient Roman amphitheatre

Sentence: The theatre group has built a vomitorium for their Roman play.

144. Astrolabe

as-troh-layb

Meaning: small devices used to make astronomical measurements

Sentence: Astrolabes were used by astronomers and navigators to measure the position of celestial bodies.

145. Furbelow

fur-buh-loh

Meaning: an older term for a decorative ruffle or frill

Sentence: Phoebe's dress was adorned with furbelows, giving it a colorful touch.

146. Baldric

bawl-drik

Meaning: a belt worn over one shoulder used to carry a weapon (usually a sword) or a bugle

Sentence: The knight's sword hung from a baldric across his chest.

147. Aumbry

awm-bree

Meaning: small cupboard or closet in church used for storing sacred vessels

Sentence: Leonard exactly knew the whereabouts of the aumbry at church.

148. Mesolithic

mez-uh-lith-ik

Meaning: relating to the middle era of the Stone Age, the period when humans used tools and weapons made of stone

Sentence: History teacher taught us about the mesolithic period.

149. Deism

dee-iz-uhm

Meaning: a religious philosophy, prominent during the enlightenment, about the existence of God

Sentence: Some philosophers embraced deism, believing in the universal creator.

WORDS OF NATURE

150. Rill

ril

Meaning: a small stream

Sentence: Hedges were put around the rill to prevent fishing.

151. Nymphaea

nim-fee-uh

Meaning: a group of water lilies

Sentence: The frogs were croaking near the nymphaea in the pond.

152. Frass

frass

Meaning: the tiny fragments of wood or plant material excreted by insects

Sentence: The frass around the tree trunk attracted the grizzly bear.

153. Verdant

ver-dnt

Meaning: a valley or countryside that is green

Sentence: Ireland is famous for its verdant countryside.

154. Psithurism

sith-err-iz-um

Meaning: the sound of rustling leaves in the wind

Sentence: As Jenny walked through the forest, the psithurism of autumn leaves created a soothing melody.

155. Abloom

e-bl-oo-m

Meaning: covered in new flowers

Sentence: Central Park was abloom with fresh flowers.

156. Riparian

ri-pair-ee-uhn

Meaning: related to or situated on the banks of a river

Sentence: The riparian vegetation along the river helped the villagers to re-build their lives after the earthquake.

157. Hummock

hum-uhk

Meaning: small, raised land in the ground

Sentence: Harry climbed the hummock to get a better view of the pond.

158. Eolian

ee-oh-lee-an

Meaning: related to or carried by the wind

Sentence: The eolian sand dunes shifted constantly under the desert wind.

159. Glade

glayd

Meaning: a small, open area in a forest where the sun shines through

Sentence: The glade was a perfect spot for our campsite.

160. Gossamer

goss-uh-mer

Meaning: a very fine, light, and delicate substance

Sentence: Morning sunlight beamed through the spider's gossamer web.

161. Noyade

noy-ade

Meaning: a sudden flood that drowns land and creatures

Sentence: The unexpected noyade from the overflowing river left the valley submerged.

162. Barchan

bar-kan

Meaning: a crescent-shaped sand dune formed by wind

Sentence: Mario and his friends were found on the barchan dunes near the oasis in the desert.

163. Beguiling

buh-gile-uhng

Meaning: charming or enchanting, often in a deceptive way

Sentence: Jane has the most beguiling smile.

164. Moraine

muh-rain

Meaning: a pile of rocks and dirt left by a moving glacier

Sentence: The polar bears climbed over the moraine left behind by the glacier.

165. Brontide

bron-tyd

Meaning: a distant rumbling sound, like thunder, from natural movements of the Earth

Sentence: As we camped by the mountains, we heard a deep brontide, as if the Earth itself was growling.

166. Idyllic

i-dl-ik

Meaning: perfectly tranquil or peaceful

Sentence: Scot's cabin on the hills was idyllic, undisturbed by the city noise.

167. Yonder

yon-der

Meaning: something far away

Sentence: Adrian and I saw the Christmas trees yonder, their peaks covered in snow.

168. Peregrine

per-uh-grin

Meaning: wandering, traveling from place to place

Sentence: The peregrine falcon hovered over the stream in search of its prey.

169. Hapaxanthous

ha-pak-san-thus

Meaning: a plant that flowers only once before dying

Sentence: The hapaxanthous agave bloomed after many years, its final act before withering away.

170. Xerophyte

zeer-oh-fyt

Meaning: a plant that survives in dry places

Sentence: Cacti are xerophytes, storing water in their thick stems to survive desert heat.

171. Scrump

skruhmp

Meaning: to steal fruit from an orchard or garden

Sentence: The children often scrump strawberries from our neighbor's garden.

172. Nidificate

nid-uh-fi-kayt

Meaning: to build a nest

Sentence: The pigeons nidificated in the oak tree in my backyard.

173. Sike

syk

Meaning: a small stream or ditch

Sentence: We need to walk over the sike to reach the other end of the forest.

174. Petrichor

pet-ri-kor

Meaning: the sweet, earthy scent produced when rain falls on dry soil

Sentence: The petrichor after the first rain made the whole garden smell fresh and earthy.

175. Moonglade

mu-n-gleid

Meaning: reflection of moonlight on water

Sentence: The moonglade on the lake shone Lacy's eyes with twinkle.

176. Apricity

uh-pris-uh-tee

Meaning: the warmth of the Sun on a cold day

Sentence: After hours in the chilly air, the apricity of the afternoon Sun felt soothing on my skin.

177. Zephyr

zeff-ur

Meaning: a gentle, light breeze

Sentence: A pleasant zephyr cooled the hot afternoon air.

178. Spoondrift

spu:nˌdrift

Meaning: showery sprinkle of seawater blown by wind from the top of waves

Sentence: Jenny wore glasses to protect her eyes from the spoondrift while standing on the deck.

179. Mote

moht

Meaning: a tiny particle or speck

Sentence: Charles tried to catch a mote of dust floating in the sunlight.

180. Sublime

suh-blime

Meaning: excellence or beauty that inspires admiration

Sentence: The sublime view from the hills gave a sense of tranquility to the hikers.

181. Lacustrine

luh-kuss-trin

Meaning: related to lakes

Sentence: Shelly likes the lacustrine ecosystem with colorful fishes in it.

182. Frondescence

fron-des-uhns

Meaning: the appearance of new leaves on a plant

Sentence: During springtime, a rainbow of frondescence envelops the valley.

FEELINGS & EMOTION WORDS

183. Velleity

vuh-lee-uh-tee

Meaning: a wish that is not strong enough to lead to action

Sentence: She had the velleity to play the guitar, but never participated in any concert.

184. Elysian

ih-liz-ee-uhn

Meaning: blissful state or feeling

Sentence: The elysian beauty of the lake made us set up our tents there.

185. Rapture

rap-cher

Meaning: a feeling of intense pleasure or joy

Sentence: I gazed at the breathtaking view of Niagara Falls with complete rapture.

186. Logy

loh-gee

Meaning: feeling sluggish or lethargic

Sentence: After taking the test for 3 hours, Shanon felt logy and needed rest.

187. Euphoria

yoo-for-ee-uh

Meaning: a feeling of intense happiness or excitement

Sentence: After winning the competition, I was filled with euphoria.

188. Weltschmerz

velt-shmerts

Meaning: a feeling of melancholy about the world

Sentence: Joshua's songs are weltschmerz-laden but melodious.

189. Leucocholy

loo-kuh-kah-lee

Meaning: a feeling of melancholy that comes from indulging in trivial or meaningless distractions

Sentence: Jane is such an introvert; she often experiences leucocholy.

190. Compunction

kuhm-puhngk-shuhn

Meaning: a feeling of guilt that prevents wrongdoing

Sentence: Marino felt compunction after lying.

191. Dudgeon

duh-juhn

Meaning: feeling of offense or deep resentment

Sentence: Moana left the party in high dudgeon.

192. Meraki

may-rah-kee

Meaning: to do something with soul, creativity, or love

Sentence: She painted a portrait with meraki, pouring different colors onto the canvas.

193. Exultant

eg-zuhl-tuhnt

Meaning: feeling or expressing great joy, triumph, or happiness

Sentence: She was exultant after receiving the long-awaited promotion.

194. All-overish

awl-oh-ver-ish

Meaning: feeling of unease or discomfort

Sentence: After staying out in the cold for hours, Polly started feeling all-overish and decided to head home.

195. Rhapsody

rap-suh-dee

Meaning: an expression of joy or enthusiasm

Sentence: Her travelogue on Italy was filled with rhapsody; she couldn't hide her excitement on camera.

---

196. Dolorifuge

duh-loh-rih-fyooj

Meaning: something that drives away pain or acts as a pain reliever

Sentence: Chamomile tea acts as a natural dolorifuge, easing my headache.

---

197. Desiderium

deh-sih-deer-ee-um

Meaning: deep sense of longing or desire

Sentence: After moving to London, Jimmy was consumed by desiderium for his childhood home in Kentucky.

198. Tendresse

tohn-dress

Meaning: tenderness or affection

Sentence: Daddy looked at me with such tendresse, his love evident in every gentle gesture.

---

199. Blithesome

blyth-suhm

Meaning: happy, cheerful, or carefree

Sentence: I danced at my cousin's wedding in a blithesome manner, amusing everyone.

---

200. Acedia

uh-see-dee-uh

Meaning: a state of listlessness often associated with a lack of interest in life

Sentence: The endless household chores filled Aunt Lydia with acedia making it hard to tend to her own well-being.

201. Ambedo

am-bee-doh

Meaning: a kind of melancholic trance in which you become completely absorbed in vivid sensory details

Sentence: I sat in ambedo feeling helpless as I could not save my bunny from the cat.

---

202. Waldeinsamkeit

vald-ine-zam-kite

Meaning: the feeling of being alone in the woods, a pleasant solitude

Sentence: The waldeinsamkeit of the forest walk was exactly what she needed to clear her mind.

203. Occhiolism

ok-ee-oh-liz-um

Meaning: the awareness of the smallness of your perspective

Sentence: In my Geology class I realized how little I know about Earth; it filled me with occhiolism.

204. Wabi-Sabi

wah-bee sah-bee

Meaning: a Japanese concept evoking a sense of appreciation for imperfection

Sentence: The cracked vase was an example of wabi-sabi, beautiful because of its flaws.

205. Timorous

tim-er-uhs

Meaning: suffering from nervousness or a lack of confidence; timid

Sentence: Leopold is a timorous creature who shies away from social interactions.

206. Vellichor

vel-lih-kor

Meaning: the strange wistfulness of bookstores, filled with old, forgotten stories

Sentence: I felt a deep vellichor as I wandered through the mahogany shelves of Grandpa's library.

207. Monachopsis

mon-uh-kop-sis

Meaning: the subtle but persistent feeling of being out of place

Sentence: At Cassandra's party, Jenny felt monachopsis as no one was playing with her.

208. Hiraeth

heer-eyeth

Meaning: a deep longing or homesickness for a place you cannot return to, or that may never have existed

Sentence: Henry felt hiraeth when he thought about his granny's home he had never seen but always dreamt of.

209. Insouciant

uhn-soo-see-uhnt

Meaning: very calm and does not seem bothered

Sentence: Jenny bathed in the rain with insouciant joy.

210. Onism

oh-niz-um

Meaning: the awareness of how little of the world you will experience

Sentence: A feeling of onism struck the Cooper family; they rented a caravan and went on a cross-country trip.

211. Enouement

en-oo-maw

Meaning: the bittersweetness of having arrived in the future, seeing how things turned out, but unable to tell your past self

Sentence: Standing at the podium for his valedictorian speech, Justin felt enouement, wishing he could reassure his past self.

212. Vim

vim

Meaning: energy and enthusiasm

Sentence: Gabrielle played every game with vim and excitement.

---

213. Yūgen

yoo-gen

Meaning: a profound, mysterious sense of the universe that triggers deep, emotional feelings

Sentence: The sunset on the hills fills me with yūgen, a sense of beautiful calmness longing for the dawn to come.

---

214. Klinomania

klyn-oh-may-nee-uh

Meaning: an excessive desire to stay in bed

Sentence: On cold winter mornings, klinomania made it nearly impossible for Goldie to get up.

215. Anemoia

an-uh-moy-uh

Meaning: nostalgia for a time you have never known

Sentence: Reading Little Women filled me with anemoia, wanting to walk through the meadows of Concord.

216. Gleeful

glee-fuhl

Meaning: full of joy and delight

Sentence: Rick was gleeful as he watched his daughter play the violin.

217. Liberosis

lib-er-oh-sis

Meaning: the desire to care less about things

Sentence: Uncle Joe's knack for liberosis has helped him recover from the stressful time at work.

218. Sonder

sawn-der

Meaning: the realization that each passer-by has a life as complex as your own

Sentence: While walking through a busy street, Jacob felt a sudden sonder, watching people busy in their mundane lives.

---

219. Chrysalism

kris-uh-liz-um

Meaning: the calm feeling of being indoors during a thunderstorm

Sentence: I felt a sense of chrysalism when my mom and I cuddled in the quilt as the rain poured outside.

220. Pensive

pen-siv

Meaning: deep in thought, often with a touch of sadness

Sentence: Fiona often sits by the window at dusk in a pensive mood, staring at the orange hue in the sky.

221. Jilt

jilt

Meaning: to suddenly reject or abandon

Sentence: Bree felt heartbroken after being jilted at prom.

222. Déjà-visité

day-zhah vee-zee-tay

Meaning: the feeling that you have visited a place before, even though you know you haven't

Sentence: As we sailed through the icy waters of Alaska, my brother had a sense of déjà-visité.

223. Evocative

uh-vawk-uht-uhv

Meaning: bringing strong images, memories, or feelings to mind

Sentence: The author uses descriptive words to paint evocative images, making his readers imagine every character.

---

224. Languid

lang-gvuhd

Meaning: lacking energy, force, or liveliness

Sentence: After a long day, Mary felt languid and wanted to rest.

---

225. Saudade

sow-dahd

Meaning: a deep emotional state of nostalgic longing for someone or something that is absent

Sentence: Leonard felt saudade when he found the college yearbook in the cupboard.

226. Fretful

fret-fuhl

Meaning: feeling or expressing distress or irritation

Sentence: Suzi became fretful at the movie theatre because of the loud sound coming from the speakers.

227. Jaded

jayd-uhd

Meaning: tired, bored, or lacking enthusiasm; having had too much of something

Sentence: After years of working at the restaurant, he became jaded with cooking.

228. Elation

ee-lay-shuhn

Meaning: a feeling of great happiness and excitement, often resulting from success or an uplifting experience

Sentence: She felt a surge of elation when she received the news of her promotion.

229. Despondent

duh-spawn-dnt

Meaning: very sad without hope or courage

Sentence: Cindy felt despondent after getting a C in test despite months of hard work.

230. Wistful

vist-ful

Meaning: longing for something in a sad or dreamy way

Sentence: My grandpa always gives a wistful smile as he watches his old videos.

231. Aeipathy

ay-ep-uh-thee

Meaning: a deep, long-lasting passion or emotional intensity

Sentence: His aeipathy for music kept him composing songs even in his old age.

232. Lachrymose

lak-rih-mohs

Meaning: prone to tears or easily moved to sadness

Sentence: After watching the movie, Noni became lachrymose and kept weeping for hours.

233. Limerence

lih-muh-ruhns

Meaning: a state of mind where someone is obsessed with another person

Sentence: Rudy's limerence for the pop star drives his mother crazy.

234. Collywobbles

kol-ee-wob-uhlz

Meaning: a feeling of nervousness, anxiety, or queasiness in the stomach; often associated with mild fear

Sentence: She always gets the collywobbles before speaking in front of a large audience.

235. Saturnine

sat-er-nine

Meaning: Having a gloomy or sullen temperament

Sentence: The old mansion's saturnine atmosphere made it feel like a place straight out of a Gothic novel.

---

236. Exuberant

uhgz-yoo-buh-ruhnt

Meaning: full of energy, excitement, and cheerfulness

Sentence: The children were exuberant on seeing the magician at the birthday party.

---

237. Lorn

lorn

Meaning: lost, abandoned, or forsaken

Sentence: The lorn puppy barked at every stranger passing by.

238. Panglossian

pan-gloss-ee-uhn

Meaning: excessively or blindly optimistic

Sentence: Despite the numerous challenges ahead, Harry's panglossian attitude left the team feeling hopeful.

239. Adronitis

a-draw-ni-tis

Meaning: frustration with how long it takes to get to know someone

Sentence: Jerry could not accept Tim as his stepbrother which filled his mom's heart with adronitis.

240. Abulia

uh-boo-lee-uh

Meaning: lack of willpower or the ability to make decisions

Sentence: His abulia became evident when he could not even decide on simple matters like what to eat.

241. Flabbergasted

fla-buh-gast-uhd

Meaning: overwhelmed with surprise

Sentence: Mona was flabbergasted when she received an invitation to spend the weekend in the Bahamas.

WORDS OF FEAR & PHOBIAS

242. Sciaphobia

sy-uh-foh-bee-uh

Meaning: fear of shadows

Sentence: The child's sciaphobia made him terrified of playing outside in the evening.

---

243. Thantophobia

than-toh-foh-bee-uh

Meaning: rare word for the fear of losing someone you love

Sentence: Her thantophobia made Lydia and her pet inseparable; she was constantly worried about losing her pet.

---

244. Thalassophobia

tha-las-uh-foh-bee-uh

Meaning: fear of deep water or the ocean

Sentence: His thalassophobia made him panic even when he was on a boat far from the shore.

245. Autophobia

aw-toh-foh-bee-uh

Meaning: the fear of being alone or isolated

Sentence: Bella has autophobia; she is always looking for people to talk to.

246. Cacophobia

ka-ke-foh-bee-uh

Meaning: an irrational fear of ugliness

Sentence: Due to her cacophobia, she avoided places where she might see things she considered unattractive.

247. Rubatosis

roo-buh-toh-sis

Meaning: the unsettling awareness of your own heartbeat

Sentence: Lying in bed at night, rubatosis kept me awake thinking about the class test.

248. Chiroptophobia

ky-r248op-tuh-foh-bee-uh

Meaning: fear of bats

Sentence: She screamed and ran away when a bat flew past, revealing her chiroptophobia.

249. Philophobia

fil-oh-foh-bee-uh

Meaning: the fear of getting emotionally attached

Sentence: After Jolie's bunny died, she developed philophobia, scared of getting a new pet.

250. Atephobia

a-tuh-foh-bee-uh

Meaning: fear of ruin or collapse

Sentence: His atephobia made him anxious every time he entered an old, crumbling building.

251. Hylephobia

hy-leefoh-bee-uh

Meaning: fear of forests or woodlands

Sentence: Because of his hylephobia, he never joined camping trips with his friends.

252. Phengophobia

fen-go-foh-bee-uh

Meaning: fear of daylight or bright light

Sentence: Due to his phengophobia, he always wore sunglasses, even indoors.

253. Triskaidekaphobia

tris-kaiˌdecc-e'foh-bi-e

Meaning: fear of the number 13

Sentence: His triskaidekaphobia made him refuse to stay on the 13th floor of the hotel.

254. Malneirophrenia

mal-nay-roh-freen-ya

Meaning: the lingering feeling of uneasiness after a bad dream

Sentence: Two nightmares in a row left me with malneirophrenia that stayed with me even at work.

WORDS OF LOVE

255. Hodophile

ho-doh-fyl

Meaning: a person who loves traveling

Sentence: Henry spent all his savings exploring Egypt; being a hodophile is giving him a hard time.

256. Chionophile

kai-uh-fyl

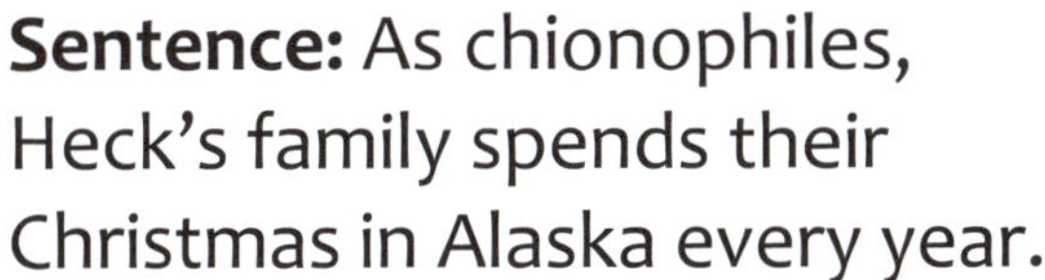

Meaning: a person who loves cold climate or snow

Sentence: As chionophiles, Heck's family spends their Christmas in Alaska every year.

257. Pyrophile

'pai-roh-fyl

Meaning: a person who loves fire

Sentence: Sheila is a pyrophile; she was fascinated with the dancing flames of the bonfires.

258. Nemophilist

nuh-moff-uh-lisst

Meaning: a person who loves forests and woods and finds inspiration in nature

Sentence: As a true nemophilist, Lisa spends every weekend exploring dense woodlands.

259. Eremophile

er-uh-muh-fyl

Meaning: a person who loves deserts or solitude

Sentence: Johnny often drives off to Mojave Desert to find some peace, which is what eremophiles do.

260. Chrysophile

kruh-sof-uh-fyl

Meaning: a person who loves gold

Sentence: My mom's love for gold jewelry has earned her the title of Ms. Chrysophile in her prayer group.

261. Pluviophile

ploo-vee-oh-fyl

Meaning: a person who loves rain

Sentence: Being a pluviophile, I find solace during rainy days; just me and my coffee.

262. Dendrophile

den-dreh-fyl

Meaning: someone who loves trees and forests

Sentence: As a dendrophile, Peter often talks about different trees.

263. Heliophile

hee-lee-oh-fyl

Meaning: a person who loves sunlight

Sentence: For the kind of heliophile Jimmy is, he should move to Florida to enjoy a warm climate year-round.

264. Lepidophile

lep-i-doh-fyl

Meaning: a person who loves butterflies

Sentence: Lopez is a lepidophile; she has created a beautiful garden that attracts thousands of butterflies throughout the year.

---

265. Homeophile

ho-mee-oh-fyl

Meaning: hypothetical word meaning a person who loves staying at home

Sentence: Janice is worried that her son is turning into a homeophile; he always prefers staying home than going out like other kids of his age.

COLORFUL WORDS

266. Vermilion

vuh-mi-lee-uhn

Meaning: reddish-orange color

Sentence: The vermilion hue over the horizon during sunset gives me a sense of calmness.

267. Topaz

toh-paz

Meaning: a golden-yellow color, gemstone

Sentence: Diana got topaz earrings on her birthday.

268. Onyx

aw-nuhks

Meaning: a deep black color; a gemstone, often with white bands

Sentence: The necklace is decorated with rubies and onyx.

269. Bistre

bis-treh

Meaning: a brownish-yellow pigment made from the soot of burnt wood

Sentence: Daddy's leather belt has a bistre tone matching the color of his shoes.

---

270. Sapphire

suh-faa-yuh

Meaning: a deep blue color; a gemstone

Sentence: Mario gifted a sapphire-studded ring on Jenny's birthday.

---

271. Cerise

suh-reez

Meaning: deep red color

Sentence: Cherry wore a cerise dress to her graduation ceremony.

272. Azure

uh-zoor

Meaning: a bright blue color often associated with the sky on a clear day

Sentence: The clear, azure sky stretched endlessly above them.

---

273. Viridian

vuh-ri-dee-uhn

Meaning: a bluish-green color

Sentence: The bridesmaids wore viridian-colored dresses at the wedding.

---

274. Alabaster

a-luh-ba-stuh

Meaning: a translucent, white mineral used in carvings; a color

Sentence: The alabaster statue at the museum glows differently under the moonlight.

275. Chartreuse

shaa-truhz

Meaning: a yellow-green color, named after a French liqueur

Sentence: She wore a vibrant chartreuse dress to the party.

276. Fuchsia

fyoo-shuh

Meaning: a vivid pinkish-purple color

Sentence: Grandpa is in love with the fuchsia flowers in his garden.

277. Puce

pyoos

Meaning: a dark purple-brown color

Sentence: My yearbook has a puce cover with glitters and beautiful stones all over it.

278. Periwinkle

peh-ruh-vin-kl

Meaning: a soft, pale blue or lavender color

Sentence: She painted the nursery with a shade of periwinkle.

279. Aubergine

oh-buh-zheen

Meaning: a dark purple color, similar to eggplant

Sentence: Cinderella wore a shimmery aubergine gown to the prince's ball.

280. Umber

uhm-buh

Meaning: a natural brown or reddish-brown Earth color

Sentence: The background umber tones gave the stage a real look of the ground.

281. Ochre

oh-kuh

Meaning: a yellowish-brown color

Sentence: The ochre cliffs of Mount Whitney illuminated during the dawn.

---

282. Celadon

seh-luh-dawn

Meaning: a pale, greenish color, often used in ceramics

Sentence: Ancient pottery has a shade of celadon taking us back to that beautiful era.

---

283. Amaranth

a-muh-ranth

Meaning: a reddish-pink color

Sentence: Janine's teacher got furious when she came to school applying amaranth color lipstick.

284. Sable

say-bl

Meaning: very dark or black

Sentence: I envy the sable of Mariam's hair.

285. Chatoyant

sha-toh-yant

Meaning: changeable color, light reflecting in a gemstone

Sentence: The chatoyant eyes of the cat glared in the night.

286. Chiaroscuro

kee-ar-uh-skyoo-roh

Meaning: the use of contrast between light and dark

Sentence: Matt uses chiaroscuro technique in his paintings.

DESCRIBING WORDS

287. Euphonious

yoo-foh-nee-uhs

Meaning: pleasing to the ear

Sentence: My aunt's euphonious voice lulled my baby brother to sleep.

---

288. Niddering

nid-uh-ring

Meaning: cowardly or timid

Sentence: The niddering soldier hesitated before stepping onto the battlefield.

---

289. Glaikit

glae-kit

Meaning: Scottish term meaning stupid or foolish

Sentence: Chandler's glaikit expression showed that he did not understand the situation.

290. Snollygoster

snah-lee-gaw-ster

Meaning: a clever, dishonest person who cannot be trusted

Sentence: Mr. Holmes cannot be trusted; he is such a snollygoster.

---

291. Rebarbative

ree-bar-buh-tiv

Meaning: unattractive, irritating, or repelling

Sentence: His rebarbative attitude made it hard for people to work with him.

---

292. Nincompoop

ning-kuhm-poop

Meaning: a silly or foolish person

Sentence: Beverly acts like a nincompoop whenever she sees a clown, trying to mimic them in every possible manner.

293. Cymotrichous

sai-muh-trik-us

Meaning: having wavy hair

Sentence: The twins in our class are famous for their cymotrichous locks.

294. Kakistocracy

kak-i-stok-ruh-see

Meaning: government run by least qualified or most corrupt

Sentence: The country was heading towards a kakistocracy due to the incompetence of its leaders.

295. Discursive

duh-skur-siv

Meaning: digressing from subject to subject in a rambling, unorganized manner

Sentence: His discursive speech left the audience confused and unsure of what his point was.

296. Simpatico

sim-pat-uh-koh

Meaning: likeable and easy to get along with

Sentence: They found each other to be simpatico and quickly became good friends.

---

297. Pusillanimous

pyoo-suh-lan-uh-muhs

Meaning: showing a lack of courage or determination; timid

Sentence: His pusillanimous behavior during the meeting made it difficult to take him seriously as a leader.

---

298. Somber

som-buh

Meaning: very sad and serious

Sentence: Her face turned somber when she realized she would not be able to attend the wedding.

299. Mumpsimus

mump′si-mus

Meaning: someone who stubbornly sticks to an incorrect belief despite being shown evidence to the contrary

Sentence: Despite the evidence, his mumpsimus attitude about the issue made discussions frustrating.

---

300. Boff

bof

Meaning: a loud laugh

Sentence: Susan gave a big boff on listening to her uncle's jokes.

---

301. Incumbent

in-kuhm-buhnt

Meaning: necessary as a duty or responsibility

Sentence: It is incumbent upon the manager to ensure all employees follow safety protocols.

302. Lugubrious

loo-goo-bree-us

Meaning: looking or sounding sad and dismal; gloomy

Sentence: The lugubrious ambiance of the woods makes me sad.

---

303. Droll

drole

Meaning: amusing in an odd way, whimsically humorous

Sentence: Henry looks like a droll little man with his red colored pointed shoes.

---

304. Rigmarole

rig-muh-role

Meaning: a long and complicated procedure

Sentence: We were tired of going through the rigmarole just to register for Comic-Con.

305. Mellifluous

muh-li-floo-uhs

Meaning: pleasing and musical to hear

Sentence: Montana comforted the kids with his low mellifluous voice.

---

306. Sagacious

suh-gay-shuhs

Meaning: having or showing keen mental discernment and good judgment

Sentence: His sagacious advice helped the company avoid a costly mistake.

---

307. Lackadaisical

la-kuh-day-zuhk-uhl

Meaning: carelessly lazy without enthusiasm

Sentence: Jerry is often lackadaisical about the parties on weekends.

308. Laconic

luh-kaw-nuhk

Meaning: concise to the point of seeming rude or mysterious

Sentence: Jester has a reputation for being laconic.

309. Lissome

lis-uhm

Meaning: flexible and graceful

Sentence: I got a lissome doll on my birthday.

310. Obnubilate

ob-noo-buh-layt

Meaning: to obscure or darken

Sentence: The clouds obnubilated the scenery when we were driving to Niagara Falls.

311. Belligerent

buh-li-juh-ruhnt

Meaning: hostile and aggressive

Sentence: Sharon was in a belligerent mood after fighting with her brother.

312. Hugger-mugger

hug-er-mug-er

Meaning: a state of confusion or disorder

Sentence: The classroom was in hugger-mugger after they announced post-lunch leave.

313. Redolent

red-uh-luhnt

Meaning: strong, pleasant smell; strongly reminiscent of something

Sentence: The garden was redolent with the scent of roses and lilies.

314. Tyro

ty-roh

Meaning: a beginner or novice

Sentence: Though a tyro in Spanish, Leonard is doing well in the class.

315. Slapdash

slap-dash

Meaning: performing work quickly and carelessly

Sentence: Steward gave a slapdash performance at the concert, leaving the audience feeling disappointed.

316. Brobdingnagian

brob-ding-nag-ee-uhn

Meaning: gigantic; of enormous size

Sentence: The villagers built the brobdingnagian statue to honor the king.

317. Bungling

buhng-guhl-uhng

Meaning: incompetently, clumsy

Sentence: Harry was criticized for his bungling in the presentation.

318. Hubristic

hu-bris-tik

Meaning: excessively proud, arrogant

Sentence: Jack supported Boris in his hubristic attitude in the class.

319. Ineffable

in-ef-uh-buhl

Meaning: too great or extreme to be expressed in words

Sentence: Mr. Green's teaching method is ineffable; everyone in the class loves him.

320. Comely

kuhm-lee

Meaning: pleasant, attractive

Sentence: Shirley resembles the comely Italian actress.

321. Clammy

klam-ee

Meaning: unpleasantly moist, sticky, and cold

Sentence: Dolphins and belugas are clammy to touch.

322. Doryphore

dor-i-for

Meaning: a person who constantly criticizes or points out mistakes

Sentence: Her doryphore attitude has made it difficult for her to make friends in class.

323. Resplendent

ri-splen-dent

Meaning: attractive and impressive through being richly colorful, magnificent

Sentence: The bride looked resplendent in the ivory white gown.

324. Winsome

win-suhm

Meaning: attractive or appealing in appearance or character

Sentence: Ana charms everyone with her winsome smile.

325. Eirenic

igh-ren-ik

Meaning: peaceful

Sentence: Her eirenic disposition helped resolve many conflicts within the team.

326. Abradant

uh-bray-dunt

Meaning: a material used for abrasion or removing roughness

Sentence: Paul used abradant sandpaper to smoothen the rough edges of his Christmas tree.

327. Labyrinthine

lab-uh-rin-thyn

Meaning: complicated or maze-like

Sentence: Barry knows all the labyrinthine streets of the old city.

328. Farrago

fe-rah-go

Meaning: a confused mixture of things

Sentence: His farrago of contradictory statements confused the cops.

329. Cacophony

ka-koffe-oh-nee

Meaning: a harsh, discordant mixture of sounds

Sentence: I could not hear her over the cacophony created by the endless traffic on road.

330. Beatific

bee-uh-tif-ik

Meaning: blissfully happy

Sentence: Newborn babies have a beatific smile.

331. Quixotic

kwik-sot-ik

Meaning: exceedingly idealistic; unrealistic and impractical

Sentence: Hanna's quixotic behavior makes her different from her friends.

332. Tatterdemalion

tat-er-duh-mayl-yuhn

Meaning: a person in ragged clothing; a shabby appearance

Sentence: The tatterdemalion wandered the streets at midnight scaring the street dogs.

333. Cynosure

Sye-nuh-shoor

Meaning: the center of attention or admiration

Sentence: The princess, in her glittering gown, was the cynosure of the Royal ball.

334. Ultracrepidarian

uhl-truh-krep-i-dayr-ee-uhn

Meaning: a person who gives opinions on matters they know little about

Sentence: Lary is an ultracrepidarian and pretends to know everything about everything.

335. Craggy

krag-ee

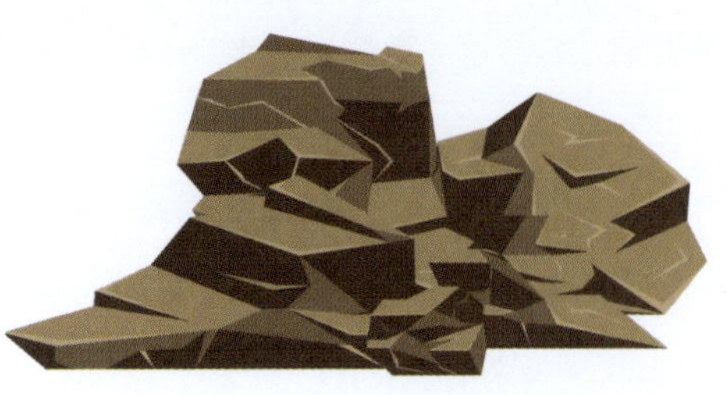

Meaning: rough and uneven, like a rocky surface

Sentence: The craggy cliff was difficult to climb.

---

336. Ribbed

ribd

Meaning: marked by raised bands or ridges

Sentence: The ribbed surface of the rock made it easy for us to climb.

337. Bristly

bris-lee

Meaning: covered with stiff, coarse hair or spine

Sentence: The doll had furry eyebrows and bristly hair, unlike other dolls.

338. Quilted

kwil-tid

Meaning: made of layers sewn together, often creating a raised, textured pattern

Sentence: Larry's mom made quilted jackets for everyone on the trip.

339. Nubbly

nuhb-lee

Meaning: having small, rough bumps

Sentence: The head of my dog has a nubbly feel to it.

340. Risible

riz-uh-buhl

Meaning: provoking laughter or amusement

Sentence: The risible acts of the clown had us laughing like crazy.

341. Susurrus

soo-sur-uhs

Meaning: a whispering or rustling sound

Sentence: Jane likes listening to the soft susurrus background sound while drawing.

342. Apocryphal

uh-pok-ri-fuhl

Meaning: of doubtful authenticity, although widely circulated as true

Sentence: Everyone believes Jester's story but it seems apocryphal.

343. Philoprogenitive

fil-uh-proh-jen-uh-div

Meaning: having a strong love or affection for one's children or for children in general

Sentence: Her philoprogenitive nature was evident as she volunteered at the local orphanage every weekend.

344. Pulchritude

pul-kri-tood

Meaning: physical beauty

Sentence: The pulchritude of the landscape took everyone's breath away.

345. Stubbly

stuh-buhl-ee

Meaning: covered with short, stiff hair

Sentence: The stubby goblins attacked the princess.

346. Pithy

pith-ee

Meaning: concise and meaningful, often referring to language or statements

Sentence: His speech was pithy and powerful, delivering a strong message in just a few words.

BEHAVIOR, MANNER & ACTION WORDS

347. Susurrate

suss-uh-rayt

Meaning: to whisper or murmur softly

Sentence: The girls susurrated on seeing the magician creating a mysterious atmosphere.

---

348. Xenodochy

zen-uh-doh-kee

Meaning: hospitality to strangers or travelers

Sentence: Ms. Peterson's xenodochy was warm, yet there was something unsettling about her.

---

349. Garrulous

gar-uh-luhs

Meaning: excessively talkative, especially on trivial matters

Sentence: Harold is a garrulous old fellow sharing stories from his yesteryears every time he comes to a gathering.

350. Grandiloquent

gran-dil-oh-kwuhnt

Meaning: extravagant in language, style, or manner

Sentence: Perry's grandiloquent speech was more about showing off than making sense.

351. Obstreperous

uhb-strep-er-uhs

Meaning: noisy and difficult to control

Sentence: The students turn obstreperous in the absence of a teacher.

352. Bloviate

bloh-vee-ayt

Meaning: to speak at length in a pompous, boastful, or inflated manner

Sentence: He tends to bloviate about his achievements but rarely gets to the point of the conversation.

353. Defenestrate

dee-fen-uh-strayt

Meaning: to throw something out of a window

Sentence: In a fit of rage, Jolly threatened to defenestrate the alarm clock.

354. Akrasia

uh-kray-zee-uh

Meaning: lack of self-discipline

Sentence: Despite knowing medicine would treat his sore throat, Timmy's akrasia led him to eat a frozen yogurt.

355. Flummox

fluh-muhks

Meaning: to bewilder, confuse, or perplex someone

Sentence: The complicated instructions completely flummoxed me, and I had to ask for help.

356. Gregarious

gruh-gair-ee-uhs

Meaning: fond of company, sociable; enjoying the company of others

Sentence: Sherry's gregarious nature makes her the life of every party, drawing people in with her warmth and charm.

357. Morose

muh-rose

Meaning: sullen and ill-tempered

Sentence: Harry became morose after he argued with his friend.

358. Pettifogger

pet-ee-fog-er

Meaning: a person who engages in petty or dishonest practices

Sentence: No one trusted the pettifogger, knowing he would use underhanded tactics to win, no matter the cost.

359. Bruxism

bruk-siz-uhm

Meaning: the habit of grinding one's teeth, often unconsciously

Sentence: Her bruxism became so severe that she had to wear a mouth guard at night.

360. Opprobrious

uh-proh-bree-uhs

Meaning: expressing scorn or criticism

Sentence: Jamie's opprobrious remarks towards Oliver were not necessary.

361. Sanguine

sang-gwin

Meaning: optimistic or positive, especially in a difficult situation

Sentence: Despite getting bad grades in Algebra, Fiona remained sanguine about the rest of the subjects.

362. Perfunctory

per-funk-tuh-ree

Meaning: done without care or interest; superficial

Sentence: Flora gave a perfunctory nod at the breakfast table.

363. Malapert

mal-uh-purt

Meaning: boldly disrespectful

Sentence: Mindy is such a malapert, having no boundaries when she talks.

364. Discombobulate

dis-kum-bob-yuh-layt

Meaning: to confuse or disconcert

Sentence: The unexpected question discombobulated Kim during the interview.

365. Ebullience

ih-bul-yuhns

Meaning: the quality of being cheerful and full of energy

Sentence: We missed Danny's ebullience at Sabrina's birthday party.

---

366. Magniloquent

mag-nil-oh-kwuhnt

Meaning: using high-flown or fancy language

Sentence: The principal's magniloquent speech was difficult to understand.

---

367. Procrustean

proh-kruhs-tee-uhn

Meaning: forcing something or someone to fit into a rigid

Sentence: The procrustean approach to teaching ignores the individual needs of a student.

368. Felicitous

fuh-lis-i-tuhs

Meaning: suited for the occasion; pleasing and fortunate

Sentence: Jack's felicitous nature gives comfort when you are tense.

369. Rapscallion

rap-ska-lee-uhn

Meaning: extremely playful and full of mischief

Sentence: The boys were true rapscallions, setting off fireworks in the courtyard.

370. Prattle

prat-uhl

Meaning: to talk at length in a foolish or inconsequential way

Sentence: She couldn't help but prattle about her latest shopping spree, even though no one was really listening.

371. Reticent

ret-uh-suhnt

Meaning: not revealing one's thoughts or feelings readily

Sentence: She was extremely reticent about her personal affairs.

372. Flippant

fli-puhnt

Meaning: not showing a serious or respectful attitude; frivolously disrespectful

Sentence: My brother made a flippant remark on Terry's painting at the gallery.

373. Agelast

aj-uh-last

Meaning: a person who never laughs

Sentence: Danny is such an agelast, coming with his grim face at every party.

374. Effervescent

eh-fuh-ves-uhn

Meaning: lively and full of energy

Sentence: The effervescent host spoke with great energy and was able to grab the attention of everyone at the party.

375. Eschew

uh-shoo

Meaning: to stay away from something on purpose

Sentence: Henry is eschewing video games during the exams.

376. Mercurial

muh-kyoor-ee-uhl

Meaning: subject to sudden or unpredictable changes of mood or mind

Sentence: His mercurial behavior often caught his friends off guard, making it difficult to predict his reactions.

377. Lickspittle

lick-spit-uhl

Meaning: a person who behaves flatteringly towards someone in authority

Sentence: Nobody likes a lickspittle who agrees with everything just to stay in good books.

378. Lollygag

lol-ee-gag

Meaning: to spend time aimlessly or lazily

Sentence: "Sunday is over, and you cannot lollygag any longer," mom yelled at dinnertime.

379. Bellicose

beh-luh-kose

Meaning: aggressive and willing to fight

Sentence: Jason is infamous for his bellicose behavior.

380. Largesse

laa-jes

Meaning: generosity, kindness in giving to others

Sentence: The homeless would benefit from the largesse of the rich.

381. Punctilious

puhngk-til-ee-uhs

Meaning: showing great attention to detail or correct behavior

Sentence: Her punctilious approach to etiquette made her a model of politeness.

382. Anecdoche

uh-nek-doh-kee

Meaning: a conversation in which everyone is talking, but nobody is listening

Sentence: The teacher punished everyone as the classroom turned into anecdoche, with no one paying attention.

383. Rectitudinous

rek-ti-too-di-nous

Meaning: morally correct behavior or thinking; righteousness

Sentence: He was known for his rectitudinous demeanor, always standing by what was morally right.

384. Maladroit

mal-uh-droit

Meaning: awkward or clumsy in behavior or action

Sentence: His maladroit attempt at comforting her only made the situation more uncomfortable.

385. Sitzfleisch

sitz-flysh

Meaning: the ability to sit still and persevere through long or difficult tasks

Sentence: Writing a novel requires a lot of sitzfleisch if you want to see it through to the end.

FOOD WORDS

386. Alfresco

al-freh-skoh

Meaning: eating outdoors

Sentence: Daddy surprised mommy with an alfresco dinner on their wedding anniversary.

387. Farro

fahr-oh

Meaning: an ancient grain like barley, often used in salads or soups

Sentence: Pam is on farro salad as she is trying to lose some weight.

388. Rind

raind

Meaning: the thick outer skin of fruit or cheese

Sentence: It is weird to see Ron eating a plate full of cheese with its rind on.

389. Zest

zest

Meaning: the outer skin of citrus fruits, used for flavoring; enthusiasm and energy

Sentence: A pinch of lemon zest to the cake mix creates magic.

390. Gourmet

gaw-may

Meaning: high quality or fancy food; a person who enjoys good food and knows a lot about it

Sentence: We went to the restaurant for a gourmet dinner on Aunt Melissa's 50th birthday.

391. Brine

bra-in

Meaning: salty solution used to preserve or flavor food

Sentence: Granny soaks pickled cucumber in salty brine.

392. Charcuterie

chaa-koo-tuh-ree

Meaning: a selection of cold meats, often served as an appetizer

Sentence: Bella and her friend shared a charcuterie board at the party.

393. Cuisinequaintance

kwi-zi-n-kwain-tens

Meaning: a blended word which means becoming familiar with a particular type of food or cuisine

Sentence: My cuisinequaintance with Mexican food was spicy yet exquisite.

394. Barm

bahrm

Meaning: the froth that forms on the top of fermenting liquids, often used in bread-making

Sentence: My grandma adds barm to the bread dough for a traditional touch.

395. Coulis

koo-lee

Meaning: a thick sauce made from vegetables or fruits

Sentence: The raspberry coulis added sweetness to the tart that Jess baked for my birthday.

396. Comestible

kuh-mes-ti-buhl

Meaning: a formal word meaning something that is fit to be eaten or is edible

Sentence: The wilderness offered few comestibles, and they had to rely on their survival skills to find something to eat.

397. Famished

fam-isht

Meaning: extremely hungry

Sentence: Albert was famished by dinnertime as he skipped lunch.

---

398. Crudo

kroo-doh

Meaning: an Italian dish of raw seafood or meat, seasoned with olive oil, citrus, and spices

Sentence: I finished the entire plate of tuna crudo as I was famished after a 15-hour-long journey.

---

399. Postprandial

poset-pran-dee-uhl

Meaning: after a meal, especially after dinner

Sentence: Dinner at Scott's house is famous for postprandial dessert.

400. Béchamel

bay-sha-mel

Meaning: a classic French white sauce made from butter, flour, and milk

Sentence: A rich béchamel sauce is the foundation of many French dishes.

401. Culinapprehension

ku-leen-a-pruh-hen-shn

Meaning: a blended word meaning the nervousness or uncertainty about trying a new or exotic food

Sentence: Rosie felt culinapprehension before tasting the food prepared by her brother.

402. Entrée

on-tray

Meaning: the main dish of a meal

Sentence: We ordered grilled salmon with asparagus for entrée at the restaurant.

403. Brioche

bree-osh

Meaning: sweet bread made with eggs and butter

Sentence: I was tired of having brioche with butter for breakfast, five days in a row.

404. Flexitarian

flek-si-tair-ee-uh

Meaning: a person who follows a primarily vegetarian diet but occasionally eats meat

Sentence: As a flexitarian, Jia mostly ate plant-based meals but enjoyed fish once a week.

405. Ballotine

bal-loh-teen

Meaning: a dish made by stuffing and rolling meat before cooking

Sentence: The ballotine of turkey was filled with creamy mushrooms and sweet corn.

406. Macédoine

mah-seh-dwan

Meaning: a mixture of diced fruits or vegetables

Sentence: Shelly is famous for her fruit macédoine; she always serves it with freshly-whipped cream.

---

407. Aromelancholy

arow-meh-luhng-kuh-lee

Meaning: a feeling of sadness or wistfulness triggered by the smell of a particular food

Sentence: The aroma of apple pie filled her with aromelancholy reminding her of home.

---

408. Lardon

lar-don

Meaning: small pieces of pork fat used to add flavor to dishes

Sentence: I ordered salad that was sprinkled with crispy lardons.

409. Artisan

a-tee-zun

Meaning: a person skilled in a craft; also refers to food or products made traditionally, often by hand, without mass production

Sentence: Manny gets bread made by an artisan from the local bakery every Sunday.

410. Aperitif

ah-peh-ree-teef

Meaning: a drink taken before a meal to stimulate the appetite

Sentence: Joe always starts having dinner with a light aperitif.

411. Frangipane

fran-jih-pan

Meaning: an almond-flavored pastry filling

Sentence: The pie was filled with frangipane and topped with apricots.

412. Chewtrospection

chi-oo-spek-shn

Meaning: a playful word which means reflecting on past meals or food experiences while chewing on a current meal

Sentence: While having porridge for lunch, I had chewtrospection, missing the meatballs we had for dinner the previous night.

413. Dredge

drej

Meaning: to coat food lightly with a dry ingredient like flour

Sentence: Emily dredges the chicken in flour before frying it.

414. Borborygmus

bawr-buh-rig-muhs

Meaning: intestinal rumbling sound caused by moving gas

Sentence: The borborygmus was loud enough for everyone to hear.

415. Flavor reticence

flay-ver ret-uh-sens

Meaning: hesitation or reluctance to try food because of its strong smell or appearance

Sentence: Jack eventually tried the baked aubergine despite his flavor reticence; he was surprised by its gooey texture.

---

416. Dacquoise

dah-kwahz

Meaning: a French dessert made with layers of nut-flavored meringue and buttercream or whipped cream

Sentence: The hazelnut dacquoise with a hint of vanilla was a perfect treat.

---

417. Locavore

loh-kuh-vor

Meaning: someone who only eats food that is locally grown or produced

Sentence: As a locavore, Jessica avoided imported fruits and only shopped at the farmers' market.

418. Nosh

nosh

Meaning: an informal term for food, especially when referring to a snack or light meal

Sentence: After the long meeting, they went to the break room for some quick nosh to recharge.

419. Epicure

ep-uh-kyur

Meaning: a person who has a refined taste for food and drink

Sentence: As an epicure, she always sought out the finest restaurants that served exquisitely-prepared dishes.

420. Slake

slayk

Meaning: to quench thirst or desire

Sentence: The cool water slaked my thirst after the uphill climb.

421. Amuse-bouche

ah-mewz-boosh

Meaning: a complementary bite-size appetizer served before a meal

Sentence: Our lunch began with an amuse-bouche of French onion soup, followed by roasted scallops.

422. Jentacular

jen-tack-yoo-lar

Meaning: related to breakfast

Sentence: Holly mostly sticks to her jentacular routine of poached eggs and a cup of espresso.

423. Bouillabaisse

boo-yah-bess

Meaning: a traditional French fish stew

Sentence: The bouillabaisse had an overpowering fragrant saffron broth.

FLAVOR & CULINARY WORDS

424. Sous-vide

soo-veed

Meaning: a French cooking method where food is vacuum-sealed in a bag and then cooked in a water bath

Sentence: The steak was cooked sous-vide for several hours to ensure it was perfectly tender and juicy.

425. Aniseed

an-i-seed

Meaning: the seed of the anise plant, known for its sweet, licorice-like flavor

Sentence: Maria said the ice cream had a unique flavour due to the addition of aniseed.

426. Cloying

cloy-ing

Meaning: excessively sweet or rich, to the point of being sickening

Sentence: The dessert was so cloying that Hui threw up after having a spoonful of it.

427. Bouquet Garni

boo-kay-gar-nee

Meaning: a bundle of herbs tied together or wrapped in cheesecloth, used to flavor soups and stews

Sentence: The chef added a bouquet garni to the pot, infusing the broth with rich, aromatic flavors.

428. Mouthfeel

mow-th-fil

Meaning: the texture of how food feels in your mouth when you eat

Sentence: The mouthfeel of the French onion soup was excellent.

429. Camphoraceous

kam-fuh-ray-shuhs

Meaning: having a strong, pungent smell of camphor

Sentence: The medicine had a camphoraceous smell making it difficult to swallow.

430. Hesperidic

hes-per-id-ik

Meaning: having a scent or flavor similar to citrus fruits

Sentence: My perfume has hesperidic scent that I find refreshing in the morning hours.

431. Dulcet

duhl-set

Meaning: sweet and soothing

Sentence: The dulcet aroma of caramelized sugar and vanilla filled the bakery.

432. Piquant

pee-kahnt

Meaning: having a pleasantly sharp or spicy taste

Sentence: Roderick likes to have his salsa having a piquant flavor that compliments the herbed nachos.

433. Rancidity

ran-sih-dih-tee

Meaning: a stale, unpleasant, and often fatty taste

Sentence: The butter had developed rancidity after being left out too long.

434. Macerate

mas-uh-rayt

Meaning: to soften or break down by soaking

Sentence: Granny macerated strawberries and apricots in sugar to makes jellies with them.

435. Crapulence

krap-yuh-luhns

Meaning: becoming sick because of overeating and drinking too much

Sentence: After a sumptuous meal of ten waffles loaded with whipped cream, I felt crapulence that made me throw up.

436. Al dente

al dent-teh

Meaning: pasta or rice that has been cooked but is still firm to bite

Sentence: Monica cooks pasta till al dente and then adds it to the pasta sauce.

437. Velvety

vel-vuh-tee

Meaning: smooth and soft in texture or flavor, like velvet

Sentence: French desserts are velvety that melt immediately in the mouth.

438. Mellow

mel-oh

Meaning: smooth and soft in flavor

Sentence: The falafel had a mellow flavor, compared to the hummus that was served with it.

439. Amertume

ah-mer-toom

Meaning: a refined, complex bitterness often found in gourmet dishes and fine wines

Sentence: The amertume of the dark chocolate balanced perfectly with the sweetness of the caramel sauce.

440. Luscious

luh-shuhs

Meaning: rich, sweet, and highly pleasing to the senses

Sentence: The luscious mangoes with sweet pulp are the perfect summer fruit.

441. Creosote

kree-uh-soht

Meaning: dark brown oil containing various organic compounds used as a wood preservative

Sentence: Grandpa keeps the bottles of creosote in the garage.

442. Bletting

blet-ing

Meaning: the softening of certain fleshy fruits

Sentence: Fruit vendor discarded all the fruits that had not softened through bletting before shipping them off to the market.

---

443. Mirepoix

meer-pwah

Meaning: a flavor base consisting of diced onions, carrots, and celery, often sautéed in butter or oil

Sentence: The mirepoix simmered gently in the pot, releasing rich aromas as the stew began to take shape.

---

444. Astringency

uh-strin-juhn-see

Meaning: the quality of causing a dry, puckering sensation in the mouth, often due to tannins in certain foods and drinks

Sentence: Darian enjoys the yeasty astringency of sourdough bread.

445. Chiffonade

shi-fe-'nād

Meaning: finely-cut vegetables or herbs used especially as a garnish

Sentence: The meatball had chiffonade of parsley and thyme.

---

446. Umami

uː'mɑːmi

Meaning: a savory taste, one of the five basic tastes

Sentence: Worcestershire sauce in cooking adds umami to dishes.

Worcestershire sauce is the name of a sauce.

---

447. Savorience

say-vuh-ree-uns

Meaning: the art of experiencing the full taste of food

Sentence: He ate the ice cream slowly, licking it with deep savorience.

448. Ambrosial

am-broh-zhuhl

Meaning: exceptionally pleasing to taste or smell; divine

Sentence: The ambrosial scent of meatloaf makes Tim hungry.

449. Tastephantom

tayst-phan-tom

Meaning: the imaginary or lingering taste of a food item you have had before

Sentence: Even days later, the tastephantom of the apple pie still lingered on my tongue.

450. Sumptuous

sump-choo-uhs

Meaning: luxuriously rich, elaborate, or magnificent, often used to describe a meal

Sentence: The royal luncheon was a sumptuous feast, with cuisines served from all around the world.

451. Hasselback

has-suhl-back

Meaning: a method of cutting vegetables or meat in thin slices without cutting through, creating a fan-like appearance

Sentence: Horton's hasselback potatoes were the talk of the party; they were crispy on the outside and tender inside.

---

452. Balthazar

b-ae-l-th-uh-z-aa-r

Meaning: an oversized wine bottle

Sentence: My dad has a collection of Balthazar in his cellar.

WORDS OF TIME

453. Eons

i-on

Meaning: an immeasurably long period of time

Sentence: The universe has existed for eons, far beyond our imagination.

---

454. Anachronism

a-naek-r-niz-em

Meaning: something belonging to a different time period than the one in which it exists

Sentence: A smartphone in a medieval film is a glaring anachronism.

---

455. Saeculum

see-kyoo-luhm

Meaning: a Latin term referring to a period of 100 years, often used to represent a generation, era, or century

Sentence: The saeculum marked a significant milestone in the civilization's history.

456. Aeviternity

ee-vuh-tur-nuh-dee

Meaning: eternal; lasting for ages

Sentence: Angels and demons have existed in the outer world for an aeviternity.

457. Tempus Fugit

tem-pus- fyoo-jit

Meaning: Latin for 'time flies'

Sentence: Latino yelled "tempus fugit" whenever she would find her kids lying around the couch during study hours.

458. Nycthemeral

nik-them-er-al

Meaning: a full 24-hour cycle, including both day and night

Sentence: The scientist recorded the nycthemeral changes in the animal's behavior.

459. Ephemeron

ih-fem-uh-ron, -er-uhn

Meaning: something short-lived

Sentence: The life span of an adult butterfly is ephemeron, lasting for only a few weeks.

460. Horology

huh-rol-uh-jee

Meaning: the study and measurement of time

Sentence: Jenny has a collection of timeless antique clocks because of her interest in horology.

461. Vespertine

ves-per-tyn

Meaning: relating to the evening

Sentence: The vespertine is Lenny's favorite time of the day.

462. Halcyon

hal-see-uhn

Meaning: a period in the past that was happy and peaceful

Sentence: My mom and Aunty Jenny often reminisce about the halcyon days of their childhood.

463. Peregrination

per-i-gruh-nay-shuhn

Meaning: a long journey

Sentence: Fiona got tired after a long peregrination in the last couple of weeks.

464. Vicissitude

vih-sis-i-tood

Meaning: an unwelcome change of circumstances

Sentence: The king's life underwent vicissitude after he lost the battle.

465. Hadeharia

heid-e-'her-i-a

Meaning: the habit of constantly talking about the past

Sentence: Sam's hadeharia annoyed his friends, as he always reminisced about old times.

466. Sempiternal

sem-pi-tur-nuhl

Meaning: eternal and unchanging; everlasting

Sentence: The Stonehenge in England stands as sempiternal, taking you back to the past.

467. Betimes

bih-tymz

Meaning: early; in good time

Sentence: Our class teacher always arrives betimes to prepare worksheets and greet us when we arrive at school.

468. Evanescent

ev-uh-nes-uhnt

Meaning: quickly fading

Sentence: The evanescent glow of the fireflies brings out the darkness of the moonless night.

---

469. Antejentacular

an-tee-jen-tak-yuh-lur

Meaning: pertaining to the time before breakfast

Sentence: Granny woke me up at dawn to take an antejentacular walk on the lakeside.

---

470. Perendinate

pe-ren-di-nate

Meaning: to procrastinate or delay something until the day after tomorrow

Sentence: I tend to perendinate my most difficult tasks until the pressure forces me to complete them.

471. Gloaming

gloh-ming

Meaning: twilight or dusk

Sentence: The gloaming filled the horizon with a reddish hue.

472. Chronotope

kro-noˌtoup

Meaning: the connection between space and time in literature

Sentence: I like reading books with shifting chronotope of past and present.

473. Kairos

ky-ros

Meaning: a Greek word meaning the right, critical, or opportune moment

Sentence: The speaker knew that kairos had arrived, as the crowd was eager and waiting for the right message.

474. Fugacious

fyoo-gay-shuhs

Meaning: fleeting or lasting only a short time

Sentence: The fugacious nature of childhood is missed when we are older.

---

475. Chronomancy

kroh-noh-man-see

Meaning: the practice or art of fortune-telling through the interpretation of time

Sentence: In the world of fantasy literature, chronomancy is often depicted as a powerful magic used to manipulate time itself.

INVENTIVE WORDS FROM WORLD LITERATURE

476. Tharn

tharn

Meaning: a term from 'Watership Down' by Richard Adams, referring to a state of being frozen or unable to move, due to fear

Sentence: Caught in the headlights of the car, the bunny was tharn and could not move a bit.

477. Squee

skwee

Meaning: a fan culture and comic-related word meaning a high-pitched noise or cry, typically expressing excitement or delight

Sentence: Moana lets out a squee every time she sees balloons.

478. Chortle

chor-tl

Meaning: a term from Lewis Carroll's Jabberwocky which means a blend of chuckle and snort, indicating a joyful laugh

Sentence: I could not help but chortle at the joke my friend told me.

479. Galumph

ga-lumph

Meaning: invented by Lewis Carroll to denote moving in a clumsy, heavy manner

Sentence: Penny galumphed up the stairs, her pet kitten following her slowly.

480. Whovian

hoo-vee-an

Meaning: a devoted fan of the television series 'Doctor Who'

Sentence: My brother is a proud Whovian; he has watched every episode of the show.

481. Malapropism

mal-uh-prop-izm

Meaning: the mistaken use of a word in place of a similar-sounding one (derived from Mrs. Malaprop in Richard Sheridan's play 'The Rivals')

Sentence: She is infamous for her frequent malapropisms, adding humor to the gathering.

---

482. Lilliputian

lili-pju-tien

Meaning: a term originated from Jonathan Swift's novel Gulliver's Travels, referring to extremely small or miniature people

Sentence: The intricate details of the artist's lilliputian sculptures amazed visitors.

---

483. Octothorp

ok-toh-thawrp

Meaning: another term for the symbol of the hash (#) or pound sign (coined by Bell Labs Engineers in 1960s)

Sentence: Social media popularised the term 'Octothorp' in recent times.

484. Quidditch

kwid-itch

Meaning: a fictional sport played on broomsticks in the famous Harry Potter series by J.K. Rowling

Sentence: Henry always dreamed of playing a game of quidditch with his friends.

485. Zephaniah

zeh-fuh-nai-uh

Meaning: 'God has hidden' which is of Hebrew origin and has religious significance as a Prophet in the Old Testament

Sentence: Grandma read the Old Testament book telling the prophecies of Zephaniah.

486. Vogon

voh-gon

Meaning: a fictional alien group known for their terrible poetry from Douglas Adam's The Hitchhiker's Guide to the Galaxy

Sentence: "Which vogon has written the poetry?" asked Ms. Potter.

487. Absurdism

ab-sur-diz-uhm

Meaning: a philosophical concept asserting that human existence is meaningless and that any search for inherent value or purpose in life is futile

Sentence: Camus' novel "The Stranger" is a key example of absurdism, where the protagonist faces an indifferent universe that defies reason and logic.

---

488. Bibliopole

bib-lee-oh-pohl

Meaning: a rare term for a bookseller, often encountered in literary or antiquarian contexts

Sentence: Harry is titled Mr. Bibliopole at the book fair as he has an impressive collection of ancient manuscripts.

489. Mimsy

mim-zee

Meaning: a word from Lewis Carroll's Jabberwocky, meaning a blend of miserable and flimsy

Sentence: Matt’s mimsy attitude keeps him from achieving his dreams.

---

490. Dormitive

dor-mih-tiv

Meaning: a concept appearing in Laurence Sterne's The Life and Opinions of Tristram Shandy, denoting sleep-inducing philosophy

Sentence: The professor's monotonous lecture had such a dormitive effect that half the class struggled to keep their eyes open.

---

491. Frabjous

frab-juhs

Meaning: a joyful, fantastic, or delightful thing, term coined by Lewis Carroll in Jabberwocky

Sentence: Today is a frabjous day; let us go out for some sunshine and joy.

492. Jabberwock

jab-er-wok

Meaning: a fictional mythical creature invented by Lewis Carroll

Sentence: The wonderland is full of jabberwocks dancing around the trees and singing in their shrill voice.

493. Brillig

bril-ig

Meaning: a term from Lewis Carroll's Jabberwocky, meaning late afternoon or early evening

Sentence: It was brillig when my granny declared that she wanted to have pizza for dinner.

494. Tsundoku

tsoon-doh-koo

Meaning: a Japanese word that refers to the act of acquiring books and letting them pile up without reading them

Sentence: His house was filled with stacks of books—an obvious case of tsundoku.

495. Quark

kwark

Meaning: a fundamental particle in physics; a whimsical creature from James Joyce's Finnegans Wake

Sentence: There were quarks all around the candy land, gobbling away the caramel candies.

496. Wumpus

wum-puhs

Meaning: a fictional creature in early text-based computer games, particularly 'Hunt the Wumpus'

Sentence: The adventure game at the fair was fun as the wumpus would come from anywhere.

497. Grinch

grin(t)ch

Meaning: a person who is grumpy or spoils the fun for others, from Dr. Seuss's How the Grinch Stole Christmas!

Sentence: Hardy is such a grinch; he spoilt all the fun at the Christmas carnival.

498. Vorpal

vor-puhl

Meaning: coined by Lewis Carroll in Jabberwocky, meaning sharp or deadly, often used to describe a powerful weapon

Sentence: The knight won the battle with a vorpal sword that gleamed in the dark.

---

499. Scrumdiddlyumptious

scrum-did-lee-ump-shus

Meaning: coined by Roald Dahl in The BFG, meaning extremely delicious

Sentence: The pie was scrumdiddlyumptious; the best Marie had ever baked.

---

500. Pronoia

proh-noy-uh

Meaning: a modern neologism found in contemporary writings meaning the belief that the universe is conspiring in your favor

Sentence: Joey's pronoia makes him a happy person.

LABYRINTHINE

PENGUIN BOOKS

Mini Dictionary of 500 FUNKY WORDS

QUINQUAGENARIAN

SAVORIENCE

A

Abloom: covered in new flowers
Abradant: a material used for abrasion or removing roughness
Absolution: a historical term in Christianity referring to the forgiveness of sins
Absquatulate: to leave abruptly, in a sneaky way
Absurdism: a philosophical concept asserting that human existence is meaningless and that any search for inherent value or purpose in life is futile
Abulia: lack of willpower or the ability to make decisions
Acedia: a state of listlessness often associated with a lack of interest in life
Adronitis: frustration with how long it takes to get to know someone
Aeipathy: a deep, long-lasting passion or emotional intensity
Aeviternity: eternal; lasting for ages
Agelast: a person who never laughs
Akrasia: lack of self-discipline
Al dente: pasta or rice that has been cooked but is still firm to bite
Alabaster: a translucent, white mineral used in carvings; a color
Alacrity: a magical quickness or eagerness to act
Alakazam: a magical word often used to signify the beginning of a magical action or to prompt an instantaneous transformation
Alchemical: involving a seemingly magical process of transformation, creation, or combination
Alfresco: eating outdoors
All-overish: feeling of unease or discomfort
Amaranth: a reddish-pink color
Ambedo: a kind of melancholic trance in which you become completely absorbed in vivid sensory details
Ambrosial: exceptionally pleasing to taste or smell; divine
Amertume: a refined, complex bitterness often found in

gourmet dishes and fine wines
Amuse-bouche: a complementary bite-size appetizer served before a meal
Anachronism: something belonging to a different time period than the one in which it exists
Anecdoche: a conversation in which everyone is talking, but nobody is listening
Anemoia: nostalgia for a time you have never known
Aniseed: the seed of the anise plant, known for its sweet, licorice-like flavor
Antebellum: existing before a war, especially the American Civil War
Antejentacular: pertaining to the time before breakfast
Anthropomorphism: giving human traits to animals or objects
Antidisestablishmentarianism: opposition to the disestablishment of the Church of England
Aperitif: a drink taken before a meal to stimulate the appetite
Apocryphal: of doubtful authenticity, although widely circulated as true
Apotropaic: magic or charms used to ward off evil or bad luck
Apricity: the warmth of the Sun on a cold day
Arcane: understood by few; mysterious or secret
Aromelancholy: a feeling of sadness or wistfulness triggered by the smell of a particular food
Artisan: a person skilled in a craft; also refers to food or products made traditionally, often by hand, without mass production
Astringency: the quality of causing a dry, puckering sensation in the mouth, often due to tannins in certain foods and drinks
Astrolabe: small devices used to make astronomical measurements
Atephobia: fear of ruin or collapse
Aubergine: a dark purple color, similar to eggplant
Augury: a sign of what will happen in the future; an omen

Aumbry: small cupboard or closet in church used for storing sacred vessels
Autophobia: the fear of being alone or isolated
Azure: a bright blue color often associated with the sky on a clear day

B

Baldric: a belt worn over one shoulder used to carry a weapon (usually a sword) or a bugle
Ballotine: a dish made by stuffing and rolling meat before cooking
Ballyhoo: extravagant promotion or publicity
Baloney: nonsense or foolishness
Balthazar: an oversized wine bottle
Barchan: a crescent-shaped sand dune formed by wind
Barm: the froth that forms on the top of fermenting liquids, often used in bread-making
Bazinga: a term used to indicate that someone has been tricked or pranked
Beatific: blissfully happy
Béchamel: a classic French white sauce made from butter, flour, and milk
Befuddled: unable to think clearly; confused or perplexed
Beguiling: charming or enchanting, often in a deceptive way
Bellicose: aggressive and willing to fight
Belligerent: hostile and aggressive
Besom: a stiff broom made out of sticks and twigs tied together
Betimes: early; in good time
Bibliopole: a rare term for a bookseller, often encountered in literary or antiquarian contexts
Bistre: a brownish-yellow pigment made from the soot of burnt wood
Blatteroon: an obsolete term for a person who talks too much
Bletting: the softening of certain fleshy fruits

Blithesome: happy, cheerful, or carefree
Bloviate: to speak at length in a pompous, boastful, or inflated manner
Blubber: to cry noisily and uncontrollably
Boff: a loud laugh
Bombastic: overly pretentious language meant to sound important but lacking real substance
Borborygmus: intestinal rumbling sound caused by moving gas
Bouillabaisse: a traditional French fish stew
Bouquet Garni: a bundle of herbs tied together or wrapped in cheesecloth, used to flavor soups and stews
Bourgeoisie: people who own capital, such as land, factories and raw materials; historically, this term refers to the middle or capitalist class
Bricolage: creation from a diverse range of available things; a work of art made from mixed materials
Brillig: a term from Lewis Carroll's Jabberwocky, meaning late afternoon or early evening
Brine: salty solution used to preserve or flavor food
Brioche: sweet bread made with eggs and butter
Bristly: covered with stiff, coarse hair or spine
Brobdingnagian: gigantic; of enormous size
Brontide: a distant rumbling sound, like thunder, from natural movements of the Earth
Brouhaha: a noisy and overexcited reaction
Bruxism: the habit of grinding one's teeth, often unconsciously
Bumbershoot: an old-fashioned word for an umbrella
Bumfuzzle: to confuse, perplex or bewilder someone
Bungling: incompetently, clumsy

C

Cacophobia: an irrational fear of ugliness
Cacophony: a harsh, discordant mixture of sounds
Camphoraceous: having a strong, pungent smell of camphor

Cattywampus: crooked, askew, or disorganized
Celadon: a pale, greenish color, often used in ceramics
Cerise: deep red color
Charcuterie: a selection of cold meats, often served as an appetizer
Chartreuse: a yellow-green color, named after a French liqueur
Chatoyant: changeable color, light reflecting in a gemstone
Chewtrospection: a playful word which means reflecting on past meals or food experiences while chewing on a current meal
Chiaroscuro: the use of contrast between light and dark
Chiffonade: finely-cut vegetables or herbs used especially as a garnish
Chimera: a thing that is wished for but is illusory or impossible to achieve
Chionophile: a person who loves cold climate or snow
Chiroptophobia: fear of bats
Chortle: a term from Lewis Carroll's Jabberwocky which means a blend of chuckle and snort, indicating a joyful laugh
Chronomancy: the practice or art of fortune-telling through the interpretation of time
Chronotope: the connection between space and time in literature
Chrysalism: the calm feeling of being indoors during a thunderstorm
Chrysophile: a person who loves gold
Chthonic: related to the underworld or deep, hidden magical forces
City-state: a term used in ancient history for a city that governs itself and the surrounding area independently
Clammy: unpleasantly moist, sticky, and cold
Cloistered: kept away from the outside world; sheltered
Cloying: excessively sweet or rich, to the point of being sickening
Cockalorum: a boastful and self-important person
Codswallop: nonsense talk or something utterly ridiculous

and untrue

Collywobbles: a feeling of nervousness, anxiety, or queasiness in the stomach; often associated with mild fear

Comely: pleasant, attractive

Comestible: a formal word meaning something that is fit to be eaten or is edible

Compunction: a feeling of guilt that prevents wrongdoing

Consanguineous: of the same blood or origin; specifically descended from the same ancestor

Coulis: a thick sauce made from vegetables or fruits

Craggy: rough and uneven, like a rocky surface

Crapulence: becoming sick because of overeating and drinking too much

Creosote: dark brown oil containing various organic compounds used as a wood preservative

Crudo: an Italian dish of raw seafood or meat, seasoned with olive oil, citrus, and spices

Cryptonym: a secret or disguised name

Cuisinequaintance: a blended word which means becoming familiar with a particular type of food or cuisine

Culinapprehension: a blended word meaning the nervousness or uncertainty about trying a new or exotic food

Cymotrichous: having wavy hair

Cynosure: the center of attention or admiration

D

Dacquoise: a French dessert made with layers of nut-flavored meringue and buttercream or whipped cream

Defenestrate: to throw something out of a window

Deism: a religious philosophy, prominent during the enlightenment, about the existence of God

Déjà-visité: the feeling that you have visited a place before, even though you know you haven't

Dendrophile: someone who loves trees and forests

Desiderium: deep sense of longing or desire

Despondent: very sad without hope or courage
Dillydally: to waste time by being indecisive or hesitant
Discombobulate: to confuse or disconcert
Discursive: digressing from subject to subject in a rambling, unorganized manner
Ditty: a light-hearted, short, and simple song
Dodecahedronalization: the process of turning something into a twelve-sided shape
Dolorifuge: something that drives away pain or acts as a pain reliever
Doozy: something outstanding or remarkable
Dormitive: a concept appearing in Laurence Sterne's The Life and Opinions of Tristram Shandy, denoting sleep-inducing philosophy
Doryphore: a person who constantly criticizes or points out mistakes
Dredge: to coat food lightly with a dry ingredient like flour
Droll: amusing in an odd way, whimsically humorous
Dudgeon: feeling of offense or deep resentment
Dulcet: sweet and soothing

E

Ebullience: the quality of being cheerful and full of energy
Effervescent: lively and full of energy
Eirenic: peaceful
Elation: a feeling of great happiness and excitement, often resulting from success or an uplifting experience
Eldritch: weird, sinister, or ghostly
Electroencephalographically: related to recording brain's electrical activity
Elysian: blissful state or feeling
Enigma: a person, thing, or situation that is mysterious, puzzling, or difficult to understand
Enouement: the bittersweetness of having arrived in the future, seeing how things turned out, but unable to tell your past self

Entrée: the main dish of a meal
Eolian: related to or carried by the wind
Eons: an immeasurably long period of time
Ephemeron: something short-lived
Epicure: a person who has a refined taste for food and drink
Epoch: a period marked by a significant event
Eremophile: a person who loves deserts or solitude
Esbat: a meeting or gathering of witches
Eschew: to stay away from something on purpose
Esoterica: things understood by or meant for a small group of people
Euphonious: pleasing to the ear
Euphoria: a feeling of intense happiness or excitement
Evanescent: quickly fading
Evocative: bringing strong images, memories, or feelings to mind
Exuberant: full of energy, excitement, and cheerfulness
Exultant: feeling or expressing great joy, triumph, or happiness

F

Famished: extremely hungry
Fantasia: a magical, imaginative world; a composition or work of art that is free-flowing
Farrago: a confused mixture of things
Farro: an ancient grain like barley, often used in salads or soups
Felicitous: suited for the occasion; pleasing and fortunate
Fey: giving an impression of vague unworldliness or mystery
Fiddle-dee-dee: an expression of mock or disapproval
Fizzlebop: a fun word to describe a lively activity
Flabbergasted: overwhelmed with surprise
Flavor reticence: hesitation or reluctance to try food because of its strong smell or appearance
Flexitarian: a person who follows a primarily vegetarian

diet but occasionally eats meat
Flibbertigibbet: a foolish and overly talkative person
Flippant: not showing a serious or respectful attitude; frivolously disrespectful
Floccinaucinihilipilification: the act of estimating something as worthless
Flummox: to bewilder, confuse, or perplex someone
Frabjous: a joyful, fantastic, or delightful thing, term coined by Lewis Carroll in Jabberwocky
Frangipane: an almond-flavored pastry filling
Frass: the tiny fragments of wood or plant material excreted by insects
Fretful: feeling or expressing distress or irritation
Frondescence: the appearance of new leaves on a plant
Fuchsia: a vivid pinkish-purple color
Fuddy-duddy: an old-fashioned, overly conservative, or unimaginative person, often resistant to change
Fugacious: fleeting or lasting only a short time
Furbelow: an older term for a decorative ruffle or frill

G

Gadzooks: an exclamation of surprise or annoyance
Galumph: invented by Lewis Carroll to denote moving in a clumsy, heavy manner
Garrulous: excessively talkative, especially on trivial matters
Geste: refers to a notable deed or gesture, often used in historical or chivalric contexts
Gigglegroan: a fun word describing a mix of giggling and groaning
Glade: a small, open area in a forest where the sun shines through
Glaikit: Scottish term meaning stupid or foolish
Gleeful: full of joy and delight
Gloaming: twilight or dusk
Gnome: a small, magical creature that guards treasures underground

Gobsmacked: utterly astonished or amazed
Goober: a foolish or clumsy person
Gossamer: a very fine, light, and delicate substance
Gourmet: high quality or fancy food; a person who enjoys good food and knows a lot about it
Grandiloquent: extravagant in language, style, or manner
Gregarious: fond of company, sociable; enjoying the company of others
Grimoire: a book of magical spells and instructions for casting them
Grinch: a person who is grumpy or spoils the fun for others, from Dr. Seuss's How the Grinch Stole Christmas!
Groak: to silently watch someone while they eat, hoping they will share

Hadeharia: the habit of constantly talking about the past
Halcyon: a period in the past that was happy and peaceful
Hapaxanthous: a plant that flowers only once before dying
Hapax legomenon: a word or expression that occurs only once in a text or book
Hasselback: a method of cutting vegetables or meat in thin slices without cutting through, creating a fan-like appearance
Heliophile: a person who loves sunlight
Hesperidic: having a scent or flavor like of citrus fruits
Hierophany: a manifestation of the sacred or divine
Higgledy-piggledy: in a disorganized or chaotic manner
Hippopotomonstrosesquipedaliophobia: the fear of long words
Hiraeth: a deep longing or homesickness for a place you cannot return to, or that may never have existed
Hodophile: a person who loves traveling
Homeophile: hypothetical word meaning a person who loves staying at home
Honorificabilitudinitatibus: the state of being able to receive honors

Hoopla: exaggerated or excessive excitement
Horology: the study and measurement of time
Hubristic: excessively proud, arrogant
Hugger-mugger: a state of confusion or disorder
Hummock: small, raised land in the ground
Hylephobia: fear of forests or woodlands
Hyperpolysyllabicsesquipedalianism: the tendency to use very long, multi-syllabic words

I

Idyllic: perfectly tranquil; peaceful
Inchoate: just begun and not fully formed or developed; vague
Incumbent: necessary as a duty or responsibility
Ineffable: too great or extreme to be expressed in words
Insouciant: very calm and does not seem bothered

J

Jabberwock: a fictional mythical creature invented by Lewis Carroll
Jaded: tired, bored, or lacking enthusiasm; having had too much of something
Jargogle: to confuse or jumble things
Jentacular: related to breakfast
Jester: a funny person who entertains often with a joke in a king's court
Jilt: to suddenly reject or abandon

K

Kairos: a Greek word meaning the right, critical, or opportune moment
Kakistocracy: government run by least qualified or most corrupt
Kenopsia: the eerie atmosphere of a place that is usually full of people but is now abandoned

Klinomania: an excessive desire to stay in bed

L

Labyrinthine: complicated or maze-like
Lachrymose: prone to tears or easily moved to sadness
Lackadaisical: carelessly lazy without enthusiasm
Laconic: concise to the point of seeming rude or mysterious
Lacustrine: related to lakes
Languid: lacking energy, force, or liveliness
Lardon: small pieces of pork fat used to add flavor to dishes
Largesse: generosity, kindness in giving to others
Lepidophile: a person who loves butterflies
Leprechaun: a small, mischievous, mythical creature from Irish folklore
Leucocholy: a feeling of melancholy that comes from indulging in trivial or meaningless distractions
Liberosis: the desire to care less about things
Lickety-split: at great speed or quickly
Lickspittle: a person who behaves flatteringly towards someone in authority
Lilliputian: a term originated from Jonathan Swift's novel Gulliver's Travels, referring to extremely small or miniature people
Limerence: a state of mind where someone is obsessed with another person
Lissome: flexible and graceful
Locavore: someone who only eats food that is locally grown or produced
Logy: feeling sluggish or lethargic
Lollygag: to spend time aimlessly or lazily
Lorn: lost, abandoned, or forsaken
Lugubrious: looking or sounding sad and dismal; gloomy
Luscious: rich, sweet, and highly pleasing to the senses

M

Macédoine: a mixture of diced fruits or vegetables

Macerate: to soften or break down by soaking
Magniloquent: using high-flown or fancy language
Maladroit: awkward or clumsy in behavior or action
Malapert: boldly disrespectful
Malapropism: the mistaken use of a word in place of a similar-sounding one (derived from Mrs. Malaprop in Richard Sheridan's play 'The Rivals')
Malneirophrenia: the lingering feeling of uneasiness after a bad dream
Mana: a supernatural force or energy believed to exist in certain objects or people
Mellifluous: pleasing and musical to hear
Mellow: smooth and soft in flavor
Mendicant: refers to a beggar, often in historical contexts, denoting a specific social role
Meraki: to do something with soul, creativity, or love
Mercurial: subject to sudden or unpredictable changes of mood or mind
Mesolithic: relating to the middle era of the Stone Age, the period when humans used tools and weapons made of stone
Methionylthreonylthreonylglutaminylarginyl isoleucine: a chemical name for a type of protein
Miasma: a highly unpleasant or unhealthy atmosphere
Mimblewimble: a magical spell or trick
Mimsy: a word from Lewis Carroll's Jabberwocky, meaning a blend of miserable and flimsy
Mirepoix: a flavor base consisting of diced onions, carrots, and celery, often sautéed in butter or oil
Monachopsis: the subtle but persistent feeling of being out of place
Moonglade: reflection of moonlight reflecting on water
Moraine: a pile of rocks and dirt left by a moving glacier
Morose: sullen and ill-tempered
Mote: a tiny particle or speck
Mouthfeel: the texture of how food feels in your mouth when you eat
Mumpsimus: someone who stubbornly sticks to an incorrect belief despite being shown evidence to the contrary

N

Nativism: a belief of favoring native inhabitants over immigrants
Necromancy: the practice of attempting to communicate with the dead, often for divination or magical purposes
Nemophilist: a person who loves forests and woods and finds inspiration in nature
Nictitate: to wink or blink, often in a secretive manner
Niddering: cowardly or timid
Nidificate: to build a nest
Nincompoop: a silly or foolish person
Noodle: a slang used for a simpleton or silly person
Nosh: an informal term for food, especially when referring to a snack or light meal
Noyade: a sudden flood that drowns land and creatures
Nubbly: having small, rough bumps
Nudiustertian: the day before yesterday
Numinous: mysterious, spiritual, and filled with divine presence
Nycthemeral: a full 24-hour cycle, including both day and night
Nymphaea: a group of water lilies

Obfuscate: to deliberately make something obscure or confusing
Obnubilate: to obscure or darken
Obsidian: a volcanic glass, often black, used in tools, jewelry, and sometimes associated with mystical properties
Obstreperous: noisy and difficult to control
Occhiolism: the awareness of the smallness of your perspective
Ochre: a yellowish-brown color
Octothorp: another term for the symbol of the hash (#) or pound sign (coined by Bell Labs Engineers in 1960s)

Oneiromancy: the magical practice of predicting the future through dreams
Onism: the awareness of how little of the world you will experience
Onyx: a deep black color; a gemstone, often with white bands
Opprobrious: expressing scorn or criticism
Oracle: a person through whom a deity is believed to speak, giving wise or prophetic advice
Otorhinolaryngologist: a doctor specializing in the ear, nose, and throat

P

Panglossian: excessively or blindly optimistic
Pannychis: an ancient term referring to an all-night feast or ceremony
Pensive: deep in thought, often with a touch of sadness
Peregrination: a long journey
Peregrine: wandering, traveling from place to place
Perendinate: to procrastinate or delay something until the day after tomorrow
Perfunctory: done without care or interest; superficial
Periwinkle: a soft, pale blue or lavender color
Petrichor: the sweet, earthy scent produced when rain falls on dry soil
Pettifogger: a person who engages in petty or dishonest practices
Phantasm: a ghost or illusion, especially one created by the mind
Phantasmagorical: having a fantastic appearance, like a dream
Phengophobia: fear of daylight or bright light
Philophobia: the fear of getting emotionally attached
Philoprogenitive: having a strong love or affection for one's children or for children in general
Piffle: nonsense or trivial talk
Piquant: having a pleasantly sharp or spicy taste

Pithy: concise and meaningful, often referring to language or statements
Pluviophile: a person who loves rain
Pneumonoultramicroscopicsilicovolcanoconiosis: a lung disease caused by inhaling very fine silicate or quartz dust
Polyphiloprogenitive: extremely prolific in producing ideas
Postprandial: after a meal, especially after dinner
Prattle: to talk at length in a foolish or inconsequential way
Procrustean: forcing something or someone to fit into a rigid
Prognostication: predicting future events
Pronoia: a modern neologism found in contemporary writings meaning the belief that the universe is conspiring in your favor
Pseudopseudohypoparathyroidism: a rare genetic disorder
Psithurism: the sound of rustling leaves in the wind
Psychoneuroendocrinological: related to the connection between the brain, nervous system, and hormones
Puce: a dark purple-brown color
Pulchritude: physical beauty
Punctilious: showing great attention to detail or correct behavior
Pusillanimous: showing a lack of courage or determination; timid
Pyrophile: a person who loves fire

Quagmire: a complex or hazardous situation
Quark: a fundamental particle in physics; a whimsical creature from James Joyce's Finnegans Wake
Quibblequack: a playful argument or squabble
Quidditch: a fictional sport played on broomsticks in the famous Harry Potter series by J.K. Rowling
Quilted: made of layers sewn together, often creating a raised, textured pattern
Quinquagenarian: a person in their fifties

Quisling: derived from Vidkun Quisling, a historical figure in World War II Norway; traitor who collaborates with an enemy force
Quixotic: exceedingly idealistic; unrealistic and impractical

R

Raconteur: a person who is skilled at telling stories in an amusing or entertaining way
Rancidity: a stale, unpleasant, and often fatty taste
Rapscallion: extremely playful and full of mischief
Rapture: a feeling of intense pleasure or joy
Razzle-dazzle: exciting or showy activity
Rebarbative: unattractive, irritating, or repelling
Rectitudinous: morally correct behavior or thinking; righteousness
Redolent: strongly reminiscent of something; strong pleasant smell
Resplendent: attractive and impressive through being richly colorful, magnificent
Reticent: not revealing one's thoughts or feelings readily
Revelry: lively and noisy festivities
Rhapsody: an expression of joy or enthusiasm
Ribbed: marked by raised bands or ridges
Rigmarole: a long and complicated procedure
Rill: a small stream
Rind: the thick outer skin of fruit or cheese
Riparian: related to or situated on the banks of a river
Risible: provoking laughter or amusement
Rubatosis: the unsettling awareness of your own heartbeat
Rune: a letter or symbol from an ancient alphabet used in magic

S

Sable: very dark or black

Saeculum: a Latin term referring to a period of 100 years, often used to represent a generation, era, or century
Sagacious: having or showing keen mental discernment and good judgment
Sanguine: optimistic or positive, especially in a difficult situation
Sapphire: a deep blue color; a gemstone
Saturnine: Having a gloomy or sullen temperament
Saudade: a deep emotional state of nostalgic longing for someone or something that is absent
Savorience: the art of experiencing the full taste of food
Schism: a split or division of a group into opposing factions, such as the Great Schism of Christianity
Schmaltz: an ancient term for excessive sentimentality
Sciaphobia: fear of shadows
Scrumdiddlyumptious: coined by Roald Dahl in The BFG, meaning extremely delicious
Scrump: to steal fruit from an orchard or garden
Scurryfunge: a hasty tidying of a house when a visitor is expected
Sempiternal: eternal and unchanging; everlasting
Sesquipedalianism: the tendency to use long words
Sibilant: hissing sound
Sike: a small stream or ditch
Simpatico: likeable and easy to get along with
Sitzfleisch: the ability to sit still and persevere through long or difficult tasks
Skedaddle: to leave hurriedly or quickly
Skiddly-boop: a phrase used to describe something fun or exciting
Skullduggery: underhanded or deceitful behavior
Slake: to quench thirst or desire
Slapdash: performing work quickly and carelessly
Snickerfritz: a silly or mischievous person
Snickerpuff: a playful way of describing a silly laugh or giggle
Snollygoster: a clever, dishonest person who cannot be trusted
Snugglepuff: something cozy and a soft hug

Somber: dark or dull in tone, or having a gloomy mood
Sonder: the realization that each passer-by has a life as complex as your own
Sortilege: the practice of foretelling the future from a card or other item drawn at random from a collection
Sous-Vide: sous-vide is a French cooking method where food is vacuum-sealed in a bag and then cooked in a water bath
Spectrophotofluorometrically: related to measuring light emitted by substances
Sphinxlike: mysterious and difficult to interpret or understand
Spoondrift: showery sprinkle of seawater blown by wind from the top of waves
Squee: a fan culture and comic-related word meaning a high-pitched noise or cry, typically expressing excitement or delight
Stubbly: covered with short, stiff hair
Stygian: extremely dark, gloomy, or forbidding
Sublime: excellence or beauty that inspires admiration
Sumptuous: luxuriously rich, elaborate, or magnificent, often used to describe a meal
Supercalifragilisticexpialidocious: something fantastic or extraordinary
Surreptitious: kept secret, especially because it would not be approved of
Susurrate: to whisper or murmur softly
Susurrus: a whispering or rustling sound

T

Talisman: an object thought to have magical powers to bring good luck
Taradiddle: a trivial or insignificant lie
Tastephantom: the imaginary or lingering taste of a food item you have had before
Tatterdemalion: a person in ragged clothing; a shabby

appearance
Tempus Fugit: Latin for 'time flies'
Tendresse: tenderness or affection
Tenebrous: dark, shadowy, and mysterious
Tergiversate: to avoid making a clear statement
Tergiversation: the act of changing loyalties or abandoning a cause
Thalassophobia: fear of deep water or the ocean
Thantophobia: rare word for the fear of losing someone you love
Tharn: a term from 'Watership Down' by Richard Adams, referring to a state of being frozen or unable to move due to fear
Thaumaturgy: the capability of a magician to perform miracles or magic
Threnody: a song or a poem that expresses grief or mourning
Timorous: suffering from nervousness or a lack of confidence; timid
Topaz: a golden-yellow color, gemstone
Transcendentalistically: deep philosophical or spiritual thought
Transmogrification: the act of changing into a different form
Triskaidekaphobia: fear of the number 13
Tsundoku: a Japanese word that refers to the act of acquiring books and letting them pile up without reading them
Tyro: a beginner or novice

U

Ultracrepidarian: a person who gives opinions on matters they know little about
Umami: a savory taste, one of the five basic tastes
Umber: a natural brown or reddish-brown Earth color
Umpty: signifies a large, indefinite number

V

Velleity: a wish that is not strong enough to lead to action
Vellichor: the strange wistfulness of bookstores, filled with old, forgotten stories
Velvety: smooth and soft in texture or flavor, like velvet
Verdant: a valley or countryside that is green
Vermilion: reddish-orange color
Vespertine: relating to the evening
Vicissitude: an unwelcome change of circumstances
Vim: energy and enthusiasm
Viridian: a bluish-green color
Vogon: a fictional alien group known for their terrible poetry from Douglas Adam's The Hitchhiker's Guide to the Galaxy
Vomitorium: entrance or exit passages in an ancient Roman amphitheatre
Voodoo: a form of magic often associated with rituals and spiritual practices
Vorpal: coined by Lewis Carroll in Jabberwocky, meaning sharp or deadly, often used to describe a powerful weapon

W

Wabi-Sabi: a Japanese concept of finding beauty in imperfection
Waldeinsamkeit: the feeling of being alone in the woods, a pleasant solitude
Wamblecropt: rumbling stomach
Weltschmerz: a feeling of melancholy about the world
Whatchamacallit: a term used when one cannot remember or does not know the name of something
Whippersnapper: a young and inexperienced person who is arrogant or cheeky
Whovian: a devoted fan of the television series 'Doctor Who'

Widdershins: moving in a counterclockwise direction
Winsome: attractive or appealing in appearance or character
Wistful: longing for something in a sad or dreamy way
Wobblegobble: a humorous term for eating in a shaky or clumsy manner
Wumpus: a fictional creature in early text-based computer games, particularly 'Hunt the Wumpus'
Wyrd: an old English concept of fate or destiny, particularly in Anglo-Saxon belief

X[illegible]odochy: hospitality to strangers or travelers
[illegible]ophyte: a plant that survives in dry places

Yerk: to move or pull with a sudden sharp motion
Yex: an old word for hiccuping or sobbing with gasps
Yonder: something far away
Yūgen: a profound, mysterious sense of the universe that triggers deep, emotional feelings

Z

Zax: an old, specialized tool used by roofers for cutting and shaping roof slates
Zephaniah: 'God has hidden' which is of Hebrew origin and has religious significance as a Prophet in the Old Testament
Zephyr: a gentle, light breeze
Zest: the outer skin of citrus fruits, used for flavoring; enthusiasm and energy
Zimbi: a cowrie shell historically used as currency in parts of Africa

GALUMPH

A quirky collection of 500 wacky, wonderful, and bizarre words that w tickle your brain and add a splash of fun your vocabulary.

From whimsical and tongue-twisting terms to words that sound completely strange, this collection is packed with delightful discoveries.

This mini dictionary is perfect for wordsmith, trivia lovers, and anyone who enjoys a linguistic adventure.

PENGUIN BOOKS